WELL DONE!

DAVE SAYS...

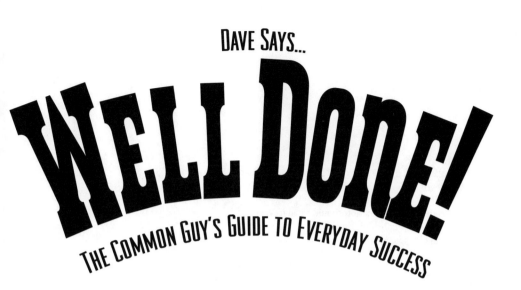

WELL DONE!
THE COMMON GUY'S GUIDE TO EVERYDAY SUCCESS

DAVE THOMAS
FOUNDER OF WENDY'S INTERNATIONAL

WITH RON BEYMA

ZondervanPublishingHouse
Grand Rapids, Michigan

A Division of HarperCollins*Publishers*

WELL DONE! THE COMMON GUY'S GUIDE TO EVERYDAY SUCCESS
Copyright © 1994 by R. David Thomas

Requests for information should be addressed to:
Zondervan Publishing House
Grand Rapids, Michigan 49530

Library of Congress Cataloging-in-Publication Data
    Thomas, R. David, 1932–
        Well done! / Dave Thomas with Ron Beyma.
           p. cm.
        ISBN 0–310–48000–0 (hc.)
        1. Success. 2. Success in business. 3. Thomas, R. David, 1932– . I. Beyma,
Ronald. II. Title.
    BJ1611.2.T47 1994
    170'.44—dc20   94-21184
                                                    CIP

In certain cases, the identities of individuals in this book have been masked by fictitious names. In several other cases, composite characters have been created to demonstrate a point.

Edited by R. Duncan Jaenicke
Cover design by Rick Devon
Cover photography by Jean Moss

94 95 96 97 98 99 / DH / 10 9 8 7 6 5 4 3 2 1

Printed in the United States of America

This edition is printed on acid-free paper and meets the American National Standards Institute Z39.48 standard.

To my wife Lorraine.
For raising a family and running a home,
for her loving harassment and non-stop support,
and for forty wonderful years and counting,
well done, Mrs. I. Lorraine Thomas!

All of the author's proceeds from this book will go to the Dave Thomas Foundation for Adoption.

More importantly, Dave has a special message to those adoptable children who have yet to find a home and love: "I hope you find a loving home real soon, and I can tell you first hand that, with hard work and values, you can go as far as your greatest dreams."

Photo Credits

CONTENTS

A First Word

Success has its ingredients—just like a good cheeseburger. You can do without the pickle or add some extra onion—that all depends on the finishing touches you like; but you *have* to start with fresh beef, cheese, a toasted bun, and your choice of fresh toppings. And the ingredients had better be of the highest quality to yield a mouth-watering delight.

I know; I'm a cheeseburger lover—and I've helped feed millions the same quality that I enjoy for well over twenty-five years now.

There are all kinds of success and all kinds of ways to achieve it. I know bus drivers who are as successful as bankers; I know anonymous computer programmers who are now more successful than some of the biggest sports celebrities. I also know glamorous Hollywood stars who are failures. I've seen good-for-nothing bums who have abandoned their families and who spend their lives with their hands wrapped around a bottle and are lucky to have two dimes they can rub together. They are just what they seem to be.

Sometimes you can spot true success. Sometimes you can't. Success can take many forms, but one thing's for sure: The ingredients of success are basically the same for everyone.

This book is about how success can be achieved for ordinary people through doing the right things. For me that includes having the proper skills, attitudes, and values.

What is the recipe for success? There is no one sure-fire formula, but I believe there is a reliable direction. As I've thought this through from an ordinary guy's perspective (which, above all else, I am; Lord knows I'm no scholar), I've come to identify twelve things—character traits, values— which I believe are the most important in pursuing that successful direction in life.

People have been making lists of values and virtues ever since the Bible was written—and probably even before then. I've seen lists that are longer and some that are shorter, but twelve feels just about right to me. So I tried to list twelve things that I felt made the most sense and have proved valuable to me in my walk through life.

My view is that you have to *show* people what success is. For example, I don't think that we really need to define generosity; we need to show what it means to *be* more generous— with our time and our talents and our treasures. And we need to stop taking the easy route—sometimes the right thing is not necessarily the easiest thing. Taking loving care of babies with AIDS, for example, may seem impractical to many but it sure is right.

Some of your favorites may not be on my list of success ingredients. As I formulated my top dozen, some of my favorites—like balance, focus, and trust—had to go, too, or be combined with other topics. I think my ingredients fall into four groups:

- *Inward* ones that have to do with getting your own act together successfully.

- *Outward* ones that are all about treating people right.

- *Upward* ones—skills you need to know if you want to go beyond just doing an okay job and truly excel.

- *Onward* ones—attitudes you need to have when you

put yourself second and other people first. I think that onward values may be the toughest and the most rewarding values of all.

Honesty, faith, and discipline are things that you must have inside of you or you'll never get off the ground. Likewise, you'll never treat people right unless you understand teamwork, support, and caring. People won't excel unless they're motivated, unless they know how to use their own creativity or to harness the creativity of others. And it takes responsibility, courage, and generosity to put other people first. The four sections of this book are pretty much arranged like building blocks that go from the simplest principles of success to the toughest and hardest ones.

Added on to these ingredients, you'll also see some other ideas popping up in the different chapters and sections. Since I'm a hamburger cook, I call these my "toppings." They're rules and outlooks that have helped guide my life—the pickles and onions of how I look at success.

Here are a few that you'll recognize as you read on:

"Anything's possible within the laws of God and man."

"You can't cut corners on quality."

"Give back—early and often."

"When you help someone, you really help yourself."

"Pay attention to the basics."

"You can't make much progress walking forward if you don't keep balance in everything that you do."

"Have a sense of urgency about most things you do, and you won't end up as the caboose."

"Focus on only one thing at a time, and on just a few things in a lifetime."

"Don't waste time trying to do things you know nothing about: either learn the basics or steer clear."

"Remember that life is short and fragile. Live it like you don't know if you're going to be around for the next breath."

"Don't take people—or our freedoms—for granted."

"Be yourself and don't take yourself too seriously."

"Do the right thing—even when it's harder than doing the easy thing."

"Put more into life than you get out of it."

These little slogans may not be Scripture, but they are some of the rules that I live by (or at least try to). I'm not perfect by any means.

If there's anything in these pages that helps you do a better job in your family, at your business, or in your community, then, hey—this book's been worth it. Bottom line for me is that I hope you find something here that you can use today—and for the rest of your life.

ACKNOWLEDGMENTS

In life, it's surprising how many teams we all belong to. My life is no different than anyone else's in that way. Some people think my belief in teamwork is old-fashioned, but I know from experience that it's the key to success. Throughout my career, I have been most successful when I was part of a team where everyone shared in the hard work, the vision, and the success.

Wendy's wouldn't be celebrating its twenty-fifth anniversary this year if it wasn't for the Wendy's team: thousands of men and women who have worked so hard to make Wendy's successful. I'm humbled when I think of how many people have taken my dream for Wendy's and made it their own. From Wendy's distinguished board of directors and our shareholders, to our employees, franchisees, and customers, each team has been crucial to Wendy's success. My hat is off to each person on the Wendy's team who has contributed to its growth, and to those who will lead it into the future.

There's one particular team without whom I would never be writing books because I simply wouldn't have the time, and that is the management team heading Wendy's—especially Wendy's CEO Jim Near, one of my modern-day heroes, our president, Gordon Teter, and CFO John Casey. Ron Musick, a key player, is a team veteran who has been with me for more than a quarter-century and he contributed his thoughts and recollections to this book.

I also want to thank my personal team including Rick Richards—my attorney and accountant—and my assistant Gloria Soffe, who earned her spurs slicing tomatoes in Wendy's first restaurant.

Any project I get involved in relies on the people who run my schedule, coordinate my mail and travel, and who always seem to have a second sense when something needs to be done. That team includes Rosi Jinkens, Angel Grubb, and Brad Treliving. Nor can I forget Debbie Bess or Marti Underwood.

I want to thank my publisher, Scott Bolinder, and his senior acquisitions editor Lyn Cryderman for their commitment to do this project, their support for it in every respect, and most especially for the prominence they have given it in their recent publishing list. R. Duncan Jaenicke—known to us all as the "Dunkmeister"—brought this book concept to the attention of Zondervan and contributed to the editing process.

My literary agent (sometimes I call him my *literacy* agent) Reid Boates gave me his usual encouragement, patience, and sage advice. After writing my first book, I could hardly imagine doing a second, and he really helped me steer this project through.

Then there's Charlie Rath, Denny Lynch, and Ron Beyma. They're the "triumvirate"—my team of dependables who have been with me on both projects. Charlie was the spark behind this one, and once again my confidant and trusted adviser in all matters. Denny was totally reliable and effective in managing the project. If Denny takes something on, everyone rests assured that it will be taken care of no matter how much effort is required. We kiddingly call Denny "Dr. Timex"—he takes a lickin' but he keeps on tickin', to paraphrase an old T.V. commercial. This book couldn't have been written without Ron Beyma. Ron used his uncanny skills as a writer to translate my feelings and thoughts into words people can put into action. He's simply the best.

Kitty Munger Thomas, an up-and-coming star at Wendy's, was the project coordinator and navigator. She brought the enthusiasm, common sense, and energy that helped keep the project on track from start to the usual frantic finish.

My family team, especially Lorraine and our five kids— Pam, Kenny, Molly, Wendy, and Lori—not only put up with the effort required to write this book, they took an active role in contributing to it and offering suggestions.

So many people helped out with the writing of this book, I'm afraid of missing someone. They are members of the research and contribution team. Some are mentioned in the book; others are not. I usually spend so much time paying attention to what's going on inside the places I'm at, that I'm not really aware of what is going on around me. The section on Camden could never have been written without the help of John Dean of the Camden Historical Society, and, most especially, Samuel Wyatt. Other "picture painters" include Father Lynn Robinson for the Memphis Cathedral, Leland McClelland for Columbus, and Norris Cranmer for Atlantic City. Joe Karam was just terrific in helping me to write about Danny Thomas.

Many of Wendy's franchise owners contributed to this book by sharing their experiences of running restaurants. Most, like Ed Ourant, are top operators. It was through Diane Dickerson, Education Programs Coordinator of the National PTA, that we were able to track down the stories of Dr. Sharon Banks and Alicia Villanueva.

Finally, there are some very special "thank yous" that I must extend. Without Dr. Arthur James and his assistant Norma Flesher, RN, we would never have been able to write the stories of Lois Gruenbaum and Denny Clark. Mrs. Jean Clark and Denny's son William were also of great help in the latter story. And I owe special gratitude to Mrs. Ruth Stafford Peale, who gave us a very special gift in her recollections of her husband, Dr. Norman Vincent Peale.

To one and all my partners, a hearty *Well done!*

As is true for most people my age, some of our closest partners and teammates have passed on. Three that were very close to me are Len Immke, L.S. Hartzog, and Jack Massey.

Len was like a brother to me. He was always supportive and really encouraged me to start Wendy's. In fact, he was the landlord of the first Wendy's. L.S. was our first big franchisee. He brought a lot of experienced restaurant operators into the Wendy's system and helped us build a lot of restaurants. Jack Massey taught me how to raise money on Wall Street and at one time was our largest franchise owner.

They've all gone on to greener pastures and I miss them. Hopefully, some day I'll enjoy an old fashioned hamburger again with them in the hereafter.

Introduction

There are two things you don't forget about the skyline of Camden, New Jersey: City Hall, which is shaped roughly like an old-fashioned milk bottle, and the RCA building with a stained-glass window showing the dog Nipper—the His Master's Voice mascot people remember from the labels of RCA Victor records. Those two landmarks still stand.

Camden is a town in the western part of New Jersey directly across the Ben Franklin Bridge from Philadelphia. About 82,000 people live in Camden, and it's a city that's struggling today. Camden has slipped quite a bit since the Quakers first laid the place out in 1773, but it is no different from hundreds of other cities in America that are dealing with the all-to-common problems of drugs, crime, and poverty.

The Camden of sixty or seventy years ago was another kettle of fish altogether. It was a bustling town whose shipyards once had jobs for 30,000 people. And if you didn't work at the New York Shipbuilding Corporation, then you probably had a job at either RCA or Campbell's Soup—the two other big employers.

The town had lively ethnic neighborhoods back then, just as proud and colorful as any in Philadelphia. In fact, Camden and Philadelphia were connected only by several ferry lines until 1926, when the bridge was built. The Italians who came from towns like Parma and Siena settled in Little Italy on South Third Street when they moved into Camden. The Germans built row houses and cottages in two districts, Liberty Park and Cramer Hill, and the two Lutheran churches even had Sunday services in German. The Polish colony was on Mount Ephraim Avenue, where you could smell *kielbasa* cooking and cheese *pierogis* frying on Saturday nights. The Jewish section sat in a district called Parkside.

For people who went out to eat, Turner's on Federal Street was the ritziest white-tablecloth restaurant in town. Some people said that the seafood there was even as good as Bookbinder's across the Delaware River in Philadelphia. And there was Weber's Hofbräu for *wiener schnitzel*.

But most regular folks in Camden went to one of the two Horn & Hardart cafeterias in town. Here you could get a complete evening meal including a cup of soup, an entree, a beverage, and cupcake for fifty cents. Those cafeterias and the automats were the granddaddies of quick-service restaurants. Teenagers in town congregated at the Tak-A-Boost soda parlor. Tak-A-Boost soda was a local non-carbonated soft drink.

To see the pride of Camden in the early thirties, you had to take the trolley car downtown and walk past the department stores and fine shops on Broadway, between Kaighn Avenue and Federal Street.

In 1932, a girl in trouble named Mollie would have walked down Broadway in Camden. Mollie had a lot on her mind and a big decision to make. She might have peered through a department-store window and stared at a wedding dress or two. Stared with some envy or hope. But maybe not.

Mollie was pregnant, and marriage wasn't in the cards for her just then. In a couple of months, Mollie would go off to Atlantic City. In a hospital not far from the Boardwalk with its rolling chairs and the movie theaters on Steel Pier, not far from Whites Hotel on the Marlborough Blenheim, Mollie would have the only child that she would ever bear—a child out of wedlock—and she would give the baby up to a couple in

Michigan and then take herself back to that walk-up tailor shop in Camden where her parents lived and worked.

Mollie passed away from rheumatic fever just eighteen years later. I wish I could have met Mollie, but I never did.

You see, Mollie was my mother.

Mollie's experience may be like America's. Sixty years ago everything seemed so right in America. Now, I hear so many people tearing it down. I'm not so sure. Certainly, there are problems. A short cut here, a fast buck there. Some folks shout about rights and completely forget about their responsibilities. But that's not true for everybody. There are many good things happening today, and I intend to tell you about them.

Now ol' Dave doesn't pretend to be able to solve all our land's problems in one little book, but I do hope that looking at the success stories of many people will help us build our individual lives successfully, and our corporate life—our national life together—will begin to turn around as well. I think of this book as a sort of guidebook by example—examples of how other people became successful in their own ways, with the hope that their experiences might suggest ways for you to become more successful, too.

I've found some answers in the way that I've tackled problems, and I'll tell you about them. I'll also let you in on some of the mistakes I've made, and a few of them have been lulus.

Wendy's, which celebrates its twenty-fifth birthday in 1994, has solved some tricky problems over its lifetime. I want to give you some examples of what our people have done—not because I think you want to open a hamburger stand, but because it's amazing how you can often use the same solutions to solve what look like very different problems.

Would you believe that watching the scoreboard at an Ohio State football game gave one of our computer people an idea that may revolutionize the way we run our drive-in windows? That's a story I think you'll get a big kick out of. But that kind of thinking doesn't just happen at Wendy's. It's going on everywhere. A person can do anything within the laws of God and man, and I'm living proof.

I'm a hamburger guy, so a lot of what I know comes from the restaurant business. But our world has a lot more to it than just business. Since I wrote my first book, *Dave's Way*, I got my own story out of the way. Doing it was so difficult that I thought I would never write another book.

So, why *am* I writing another one? Because there's a great story to tell, and it's not about me. In fact, all my life, what has really interested me is *other* people's stories. Hopefully their stories will encourage you. They are the folks who are doing things right, and that's why I admire them. What the stories in this book have to offer—as I see it—is *inspiration*. If they give you a lift, if they give you confidence that you can do it—then I've done what I set out to do.

So I have a story about a high-school principal who's reaching parents in a new way, but a way that's as obvious as the nose on your face; about a lady bus driver who has adopted eleven special-needs children and who has guided them so well that their names ended up on the honor roll; about people who, although their own houses and cars were blown away by a hurricane, still found it in their hearts to help a community in the wake of a storm; about a blind man's determination to be an entrepreneur; about a youngster whose hobby was to build bikes out of old used parts and give them to poor children; about volunteers who are milking the system the right way to make sure kids can go to college; and about a couple with the courage to adopt, not one, but four little babies born to HIV-positive mothers—victims of a terrible disease that kids in cradles sure had no part in getting.

The way that I see it, there is a big Network of Goodness made up of thousands and thousands of people. They deserve a hand, and we deserve to know about them.

We talk about moral decline today. Tell me about it. I was a product of moral decline that resulted when my mother Mollie had me out of wedlock in New Jersey. There's no reason in the world that a dirt-poor kid like me with a jumbled home life who dropped out of school should have made it, but I did— at least in some ways. And if I can, you can. Anybody can.

If you keep your eye on the main things, the plain things in life, and do them well, you can have the success you desire.

PART ONE

INWARD: GETTING YOUR OWN ACT TOGETHER

Success starts inside. Unless your own attitude and beliefs are right, you can never be a success in the world around you. That goes for being successful in raising your family, helping to lead your church or synagogue, or just makin' a buck.

People never really have their act together unless three things are true about them: They are honest, they believe in something, and they have good, basic discipline.

HONESTY

Honesty isn't black and white. In fact, many good people may look at honesty backwards: They think that it's okay if they don't come forward with the whole truth until someone challenges them with the right questions. Honesty doesn't mean hiding in the weeds; it means stepping out and telling the truth. Honesty means being sincere. It also means being fair in your deals and agreements. Honesty and integrity are twins for me; not quite identical, but pretty close. You have to have values to be honest. That's why honesty has to be my number-one ingredient for success.

My daughter Molly is a pretty good businessperson. She built up a photo-developing company on her own into a pretty big-scale operation, sold it, and is now in the restaurant industry with her husband Chuck as a Wendy's franchisee. If you ask her what the most important thing is that she learned from being in business for herself, she'll tell you flat out that you have to be honest, deliver what you promise, and work with your team. In photo developing, people expect to have their order right and ready exactly when it's promised. It's not much different in quick-service restaurants either. Molly can't imagine people being successful working with each other unless they are honest, and especially unless the boss is honest. I can't either. First things first, nothing can come before honesty in this book (or in any other book, for that matter).

WHAT YOU SEE IS WHAT YOU GET

If I really believe in honesty, the first thing that I have to do is to tell you what you are getting—and not getting. Those of you who are reading this book may not have read my autobiography, *Dave's Way*. I think that I owe you a little background as to who exactly I am. Here's a quick summary.

I started Wendy's International in 1969, and today I'm the senior chairman of a pretty big business. When radio and T.V. talk show host Larry King asked me if Wendy's was third in size compared to the other quick-service chains, I emphasized that, although McDonald's and Burger King currently have more outlets than we do, we are first in quality, and I truly, truly believe that.

Being Senior Chairman means that the company has a really qualified guy running the day-to-day show as official chairman. His name is Jim Near, and he's the best. Since a senior chairman doesn't have to sit in so many meetings or have to scribble a bunch of memos, he generally has time to focus on special areas of the business. That's why you see me in so many Wendy's TV commercials. The money I make acting (if you can call it that) goes to kids' causes.

But let's begin at the beginning. As I say, I was born out of wedlock in New Jersey in 1932; a Michigan couple adopted me just after I was born. But my adoptive mother died when I was only five, and I had the wonderful good fortune of an adoptive grandmother—Minnie Sinclair—really looking out for my welfare and shaping my beliefs on life. Although I was lucky that my adoptive father kept me with him, most of my younger years were spent in trailers and modest apartments as he moved around, tracking down work and going through two other marriages. It wasn't an easy life by any means, but I survived.

I started working in the restaurant business full-time when I was only twelve, at the Regas Restaurant in Knoxville, Tennessee. The owners of the restaurant where I worked, Frank and George Regas, were my first mentors. I adopted

Frank, George, and their workers as my family. Even though at first they didn't know how young I was, they took me under their wing and taught me a very important lesson: as long as you try, you can be anything you want to be. They were immigrants who loved this country and really steered me toward the values I still hold to this day.

When my family moved to Fort Wayne, Indiana, so that my adoptive dad could find work, I got a job at the Hobby House Restaurant working for Phil Clauss. Phil was another important mentor, and I felt adopted by his workers. Because I worked long hours, I dropped out of high school when I was fifteen. That was a big mistake, but by then I had left my family and was living at the YMCA.

At eighteen I enlisted in the army and was lucky enough to become a sergeant who worked at an Enlisted Man's Club while I was stationed in Germany. When I got out of the service, I went back to the Hobby House. Not long after my return, I met Lorraine Buskirk. I was hooked from that moment on! Tying the knot with her was one of the better things I did in my life.

About that time, I also got to know Colonel Harland Sanders pretty well. The Colonel was franchising his Kentucky Fried Chicken idea to restaurants that were already up and running at the time—selling his pressure cookers and his blend of spices and herbs out of the back of his car.

In 1962 I got the chance to move to Columbus, Ohio, to see if I could turn around four failing Kentucky Fried Chicken restaurants. The Colonel and others told me I was dumb to try, but I did it anyway. It worked. I became an on-paper millionaire as a result and then sold out my interest, becoming rich enough (and whacko enough) to build a swimming pool in our backyard in the shape of a chicken.

Even though I didn't technically have to work anymore, retirement wasn't my thing—especially since I was still in my thirties. I always loved hamburgers and really wanted to start a super, old-fashioned hamburger restaurant. That was the birth of Wendy's in 1969. Wendy's is named after our second youngest child, and yes, she really does have red hair . . . and really did wear it in pigtails back then.

At press time for this book, Wendy's was on track to become a $5 billion global company in sales, and it makes a good net profit. As for my role, I pay attention to what's happening in the company but try not to meddle. I'm not anything super special. I make a few commercials, help build awareness for adoption, like to boat and whack some golf balls around the links. That's all, folks!

ADOPTION OUT IN THE OPEN

Honesty is going out of your way to tell people the truth, even when it would be easy not to. Honesty can be a super-tough problem when it comes to adoption. Sometimes people avoid telling the truth to kids and have the best intentions in the world, but it just doesn't work out the way they plan.

Actor Lee Majors and I have gotten to be pretty good friends. Lee has been the hit on a number of T.V. series such as *The Big Valley* and *The Fall Guy*—but most everyone remembers him as Colonel Steve Austin in *The Six Million Dollar Man*. (Coming from the world of 99-cent hamburgers, I call him the "$5.9 million man," and I keep telling him, "Lee, you just don't have that value pricing straight yet.") He has a kind of quiet confidence to him, but his beginnings were tougher than he even knew for a very long time.

Lee had very loving parents. They were not his birth parents, however. His birth father was killed in an accident in the steel mill where he worked when Lee's mother was in her eighth month of the pregnancy. Tragedy took its second awful toll when Lee was only sixteen months old, when Lee's mother became the victim of a drunk driver.

He grew up in a little mountain town in Kentucky. From his first memories, Lee just assumed that the aunt and uncle who raised him were his natural parents. But as he grew up, he knew something was unusual because an older brother and sister were being raised in different households with other families. One day at the age of twelve he was, as he puts it, "somewhere I wasn't supposed to be"—rummaging around in the family cedar chest. There he found press clippings that explained what had happened to his birth parents.

What he learned became a watershed in his life. He never told his adoptive mother about the clippings, but looking back, Lee says knowing he was adopted led him as a youngster to some strange conclusions. For example, Lee's older stepbrother was sixteen at the time and had a driver's license and permission to drive the family car. But back then, Lee figured that the sixteen-year-old had these privileges because he was the real son in the family—not because his stepbrother was sixteen. Learning about his real roots also led Lee to think that he was a burden. That may have had a good side because Lee got a job as a grocery store box boy when he was pretty young and learned the tough lessons early on, building the will to win into his life. He later became such a terrific football player that he went on to win a college football scholarship.

Still, Lee looks back on learning the news of his adoption so late in life with real disappointment and regret. He doesn't resent his adoptive mother for not telling him he was adopted—she is still alive and makes her home in that same small Kentucky town today—but he does feel that it probably got in the way of closeness with his adoptive parents. What she did wasn't dishonest, and she did it for the best of reasons; but not giving Lee the truth early had a detrimental effect for life.

Lee strongly believes that children who are adopted should be told as soon as they can understand the concept. Finding out on their own, as he did, is the worst possible way to learn they're adopted.

Hiding the truth about adoption in a family can quietly do its harm to the birth siblings as much as to the adopted ones. Another friend of mine is fifty-three years old. It took his family until this ripe ol' age to finally tell the family secret that his brother—I'll call his brother "Willie"—was adopted. Willie had known for the last ten years, but his adoptive mother made him promise not to reveal the facts to any of her other children. Willie's birth mother had dropped her baby off at the convent, as was the custom in those days for a Catholic woman giving up a baby. It was the kind of story people kept hushed up.

Willie left home when he was sixteen and was always something of a loner. He looked different than his siblings. He was musical and nobody else in the family was. He even joked as a youngster that he was probably adopted because he seemed so different. The real story came out for the rest of the family only when Willie's birth mother—whom he tracked down eight years ago—recently became gravely ill.

For most of their adult lives, Willie was never very close to his brothers and sisters—though he became closer after they found out. At first he felt that he was an outsider and then he knew that he was. Would life have been a lot simpler if all the kids knew the truth at an earlier age? Would the whole family have been closer? My guess is yes to both questions.

Maybe we have to get over the idea that adopted children should blend in with their parents. Even look pretty much like them if things can be arranged. People aren't hatched; they are what they are. The idea is to give kids love and a home—not to coordinate their hair and their eyes with the parents' as if trying to match up a replacement piece of upholstery.

I wasn't always so front-and-center about being adopted. I would kind of let it trickle out at Wendy's management meetings that I was adopted. These talks mostly centered on the theme "If I Can Make It You Can Too," but sometimes—when I was feeling kind of timid—I'd forget to mention the fact that I was adopted.

One day, a young African-American manager buttonholed me and said, "Dave, when you gave your speech today, you left out the part about being adopted. Why did you do that? I always related to that because I was adopted myself."

That comment hit home for me. After that speech, I always asked two questions in the talks I gave about responsibility in life and doing the right thing. The first was, "How many of you remember the fathers and mothers who gave birth to you?" Nearly everybody raised his or her hand. The second question I asked was, "How many of you never met the father and mother who gave birth to you?" Maybe just one or two in the audience would raise their hand along with me. I was "out of the closet" and proud to be. Doesn't everybody deserve that chance?

HONEST TO GOODNESS

Joyce Chalmers is the area representative of the Durham, North Carolina, Christian Women's Club. She is very active in her Evangelical church and the Stonecrost Christian Women's Club. She says that her number-one job is being a homemaker. But you don't have to talk to Joyce for long to learn that the first duties of being a homemaker aren't baking, knitting, and laundry.

What's the hardest part of being a homemaker or parent? Joyce will tell you that it is preparing your children for life . . . and for death. Sounds odd, doesn't it, to put an equal emphasis on death along with life? But do some thinking about it. If we're honest about how we live, the first thing we have to be honest about is that we aren't going to be here forever.

These insights came upon Joyce after a tragic moment in her life. While the family was on vacation, Shawn, the youngest of the family's three sons, drowned. So the family talked a great deal about death and its meaning in terms of their faith. Shawn's death made her and her husband work and pray extra hard to ask God's guidance for the upbringing and beliefs of their other two sons.

Maybe the most important thing that the tragedy of Shawn's death taught the Chalmers family was that parents' values have to be both real and believable for kids to accept them. I'm not talking about sounding sincere. What I mean is really "walking your talk" by sticking to your teachings in what you *do*, not just in what you say. Shawn's brothers asked themselves: *Do our parents truly believe that there is a good purpose to life, if something like this drowning can happen?* As Joyce and her family worked through the loss of their son and brother, they became closer than before, and more sure of their spiritual and family values.

Well done, Joyce Chalmers!

HONEST ROOTS, HONEST RULES

One of the things I'm proudest of in my career is that I couldn't have found a better CEO than Jim Near. Upbeat, innovative, creative, loyal—he's the finest CEO in the restaurant business and has won almost every major award that the industry has to offer. Yet Jim is the first to share the spotlight and the credit with those around him. Everybody who knows him says he's naturally modest, but Jim would say that he's just being honest, and the credit really belongs to other people.

I've always been interested in how successful people got to be successful, so I've asked myself plenty of times: *Just how did Jim Near get to be Jim Near?* I think the best answer is that he came from honest roots and grew up by honest rules. Jim's story really begins with the influence of his family and his dad, Don. If you ask Jim to describe his family, he will tell you that they are God-fearing Christians. Jim's dad was born in 1913, a time when people in America focused on opportunities and not entitlements. Even though he started out with nothing, Don worked hard and was finally able to buy his own restaurant.

As a youngster growing up in Columbus, Ohio, Jim remembers he learned some of his most important lessons when his dad would come home from the restaurant after work. Standing by the sink with his wife Helen in the family kitchen at about eight or nine in the evening, Don Near would give his views to Jim and the family about hardworking, clean-cut employees in the restaurant who were doing a good job and those who weren't doing the job that they should. One of his classic comments was, "Some people say. Some people do."

Early each Sunday morning, Don and Jim would go down to the restaurant and Jim would watch his dad mop and polish the floors and wax the linoleum counters with a passion. Jim's dad felt that he had an obligation to the customers, a responsibility to them that was all part of giving the customer honest value. Later, when Jim was thirteen or fourteen and got his own first job in a diner run by an Italian gentleman, the owner told him to "wipe things down." The owner told Jim's dad that he had never seen a kid clean so hard. Jim's eyes would light up when he saw stainless-steel fixtures because he knew that he could make them shine and sparkle. Some people saw drudgery. Jim saw opportunity.

In April 1954, Roy Tuggle and Everett Burt hired young Jim to be the set-up boy at their restaurant—the Burger Boy Drive-In in Columbus. Jim started out at minimum wage (I've been told that *fifty percent* of all CEOs began their working careers earning minimum wage), but he dug in and worked hard setting up trays for this booming business. By the end of the 1950s as many as thirty-five carhops worked on any given Saturday night, serving 365 parking spots. The Burger Boy Drive-In grew to be the United States' second-largest drive-in and a huge success for Everett and Roy.

Roy Tuggle became Jim's mentor and taught him some lessons about honesty in the restaurant business. (For young people not lucky enough to have parents like Don and Helen Near, finding an outside mentor is another great way to build roots to the right values. Jim would be the first to say that he was lucky enough to have both.) Jim still remembers how Roy would take new hires into the walk-in coolers and show them how the ground beef had to feel and look fiery red and smell fresh. He would have them listen to the crackle when he broke open a head of dew-fresh lettuce. Through touch, sight, smell, and sound, Roy taught his employees how to tell if they were being absolutely honest about the freshness and the quality of the food being served.

Roy, Jim says, would be a holy terror if anybody got in the way of serving customers right. If the bun man delivered buns that had unbaked flour on the heel or if the chicken man delivered birds that weren't exactly right, full crates could easily end up back in the parking lot by the delivery trucks.

Jim learned a great deal from Roy as his mentor, and, at the same time, they developed a deep friendship with and respect for each other. As much as he loved the restaurant business, Jim went on to Hanover College after finishing high school. Two years later Roy bought Everett's interest in the drive-in and became the sole owner. After Jim graduated from Hanover in 1960, he headed to Fort Knox to fulfill his military obligations. It was during Jim's tour that Roy Tuggle convinced him to come back and work full time when he was out of the service. Roy and his new partner, Milt Lustnauer, had a great idea for a restaurant concept they wanted Jim to manage. Roy wanted to get started right away because a new chain named McDonald's was coming to town.

In June 1961, Jim, Roy, and Milt opened Burger Boy Food-O-Rama at the corner of Central and Mound Streets in Columbus. Hamburgers sold for fifteen cents. By October of 1969, Burger Boy Food-O-Rama—which had shortened its name to BBF—had grown to forty-nine restaurants in three states!

What happened next was one of the best lessons about honesty Jim ever learned, and, for that matter, that I ever learned, too. When Roy and Milt decided to sell the business to Borden for $10.5 million in 1969, it was clear to them that Jim had been the real "glue" that held BBF together and put the chain on the map, but he was just an employee, not one of the owners. So one day, while Roy and Jim were driving down the freeway, Roy told him about the planned sale and asked him if he wanted to be a millionaire. Roy explained that he and Milt wanted to make sure Jim was taken care of in the deal they were making with Borden, and that meant a gift of one million dollars.

Jim and his wife Nancy talked and talked about Roy's offer that night and what it meant. Jim put it this way: "It was sincerely the height of mixed emotions for me. I was working in a business that I loved and with a man for whom I had tremendous respect. Now I had to leave Roy. On the one hand the gift was overwhelming. On the other hand, it was frightening to go on to a completely new situation." The security of the million dollars meant a lot to Jim and Nancy, but the money never changed their values one iota. Jim went on to Borden and gained valuable experience, but the entrepreneurial spirit overtook him. He became a Wendy's franchisee and went on to build over forty restaurants before becoming our president in the late '80s and then moving on to become CEO. Jim has revitalized the business, bringing back a clear focus to Wendy's.

Roy didn't have to do what he did for Jim, and that has always impressed me. But honesty has a way of coming back and rewarding itself. There wasn't any written contract, just person-to-person trust. Jim calls it the honesty of a handshake, the integrity of a look in the eye. Roy was just recognizing what Jim had done. Today Jim is as fair in dealing with people as Roy was with him. Being honest about what you owe people when you don't have to be: that's big-time honesty to me.

BETTER TO BE OBVIOUS—AND BODIES GENERALLY ARE

Honesty should be obvious. I think that it takes guts sometimes to be obvious. I know people who'll come up to me and say, "Dave, that's a really interesting shirt you're wearing." I don't know if they are looking to buy one and want to know what store to shop at or if they think it's the funniest thing since Minnie Pearl showed up at prayer meeting with a marked-down price tag dangling from her hat. I hate vague, noncommittal remarks like that. If you have an opinion, spit it out.

America has come a long way toward making sure people get treated fairly and politely, and I think that's great, because I can remember when bigoted, unkind remarks were commonplace. Sometimes, though, I think we go overboard, especially as far as this "politically correct" stuff goes. Recently I gave a speech to an audience in a medium-sized town. My first comment was, "Wow! It's great to be in this city. As I look around the audience, I must tell you that there are so many beautiful ladies here this morning." It was true. I didn't know it at the time, but I had just shoved my foot ankle-deep into my mouth.

When I finished my speech, the mayor of the town, a woman, went up to the microphone and said something like, "Dave, it's nice that you made the compliment about women here being attractive, but you also should have said they were intelligent."

I immediately returned to the microphone and said, "Mayor, I thought that was a given."

In a way, my experience was funny. In another way it's pretty sad, because it's getting harder and harder to say things and have them accepted at face value anymore. But it's not so sad that I can't smile about it.

Nan Keohane, President of Duke University, is a super-bright lady. She was an undergrad at Wellesley, did her graduate work at Yale, and taught at both Yale and Swarthmore. (My track is a little more humble, with my doctorate coming from the Pantry League, not the Ivy League.)

Nan is an honest person, and she has some views about honesty that are better than any I could put into words. She thinks that successful people—especially leaders—have to set an example of honesty among those around them: "If you hedge the truth yourself, it's hard to persuade others that you mean what you say when you ask for honesty from them. If you have to talk with someone about his or her performance on the job, you may want to do it in private. Otherwise be open in all your dealings."

Let's say that you're in charge of a meeting or a committee, and you really want to get people to open up and speak their minds. Just how do you do that? Nan says that she's learned one answer from experience that seems to work: "Say something yourself that's perfectly straightforward. Within the next few minutes, it's almost like this liberating wind begins blowing through the group and somebody says, 'Well, since we're being candid . . .' and then puts forward this wonderful idea."

Seeing is believing in more ways than one when it comes to honesty. It's always harder to deal with people whom you can't see. If you're trying to get the honest scoop from other people, your odds are almost always better if you do it in person—especially if you don't know the other person all that well. So Nan Keohane has a pet peeve about modern life: telephone meetings. The way she puts it, it's too hard to read the body language and all the other little cues when you're talking with "ghosts" on the other end of the phone line.

Some people will tell you that body language isn't important. That's a lot of hooey. Let me tell you a true story that took place a few years back in a restaurant. A teenage girl named Kandy, who had been adopted about a year before, was invited to lunch in a restaurant by her birth father. Just the two of them would be there. Kandy hadn't seen her birth father for some time because he was cooling his heels in prison.

Her adoptive parents were a little scared about letting this meeting happen. They were thinking, *Here we've given this girl our love and a home and all. What if she really hits it off with her biological dad and wants to leave us for him?*

Well, the lunch went just fine but Kandy didn't eat hardly anything because they were so busy talking. Instead of eating, she was asking lots of things like, "What did I look like as a baby?" which is pretty common for adopted kids because many of them don't have any baby pictures of themselves. The discussion was totally upbeat, but Kandy was still sizing up her biological dad very carefully.

When the time for lunch was over, Kandy's adoptive parents came to pick her up. Then something pretty special happened. Kandy had barely touched her adoptive father during the year they had been together, but she stood up as soon as she saw him coming and linked her arm inside of his. "Papa," she said, grabbing her doggie-bag of leftovers, "take me out to the parking lot. I want to put my lunch in the car."

This fifteen-year-old girl had just voted her mind with two short sentences and the way she hooked her arm. In five seconds, she told three adults who she thought her parents were for the future. Body language talks big time.

FAITH

Your convictions are what you believe in, and your faith is the strength you have to go on believing, even when those convictions are challenged. My own personal convictions were set for life when I was baptized in the waters of Michigan's Gull Lake and accepted Jesus into my heart. Even though I am a Christian, I respect people of other beliefs who have convictions and faith every bit as heartfelt as mine. There are also people who have convictions and faith who are basically negative. You see that in some cults and radical political groups. But the way I look at it, convictions and faith don't amount to much unless they have a positive message and a positive goal. Most of all, you have to live out your faith: Don't wear it on your shirtsleeve. Instead, roll up your shirtsleeves and do something about what you believe in!

When I was eleven years old, my adoptive grandmother, Minnie Sinclair, took me to Gull Lake during the summertime to be baptized by immersion. Gull Lake is in western Michigan, near Kalamazoo, where Calvary Church once stood. Gull Lake's deep blue water was surrounded by big beautiful cottages back then. I really felt that I was accepted by God when I was baptized. But what I remember most about my baptism was that my Grandma Minnie took me there. For her, Christianity meant more than doctrine, which of course is important; it meant working hard in a restaurant, seeing to the lodgers she rented rooms to, tending a big garden and doing the canning, and sloppin' the hogs every morning. At night she'd listen to gospel radio out of Chicago and on Sundays before church we'd listen to shows like the Cato Tabernacle out of Indianapolis. The public praying and singing part of her faith might not have stuck with me all that much, but I got baptized into the roll-up-your-shirtsleeves kind of faith that Grandma Minnie held. And I believe in it to this day.

SHIRTSLEEVES CHRISTIANITY

People sometimes ask me what I felt like whenever things got really bad in my life. The truth is that I generally don't remember. Sure, I've been rejected by people . . . and had my share of business successes and failures . . . and was worried when one of the kids was sick or maybe having trouble in school.

When those kinds of things happen, I kind of go on automatic pilot. I try to simplify the problem and see who I need to help me get it solved. I would be stretching the truth if I told you that I consistently turn to Scripture, pray a lot, or have long conversations with God about my problems. I may whisper a short prayer or two in a crisis, but mostly I save my prayers for saying, "Thank you, God." In times of stress, I just want to get the problem behind me and go on to something happier. I guess I'm like most Christians in that sense. I know God is with me in the bad times as well as the good, but still I behave better in positive, happier situations than in miserable ones. That's my kind of faith.

Maybe I'm a freeloader when it comes to prayer and reflection and things like that. Many people have come up to me—especially since my work on behalf of adoption started—who say that they are going to remember me in their prayers, and, well, I take them seriously since I figure we all need as much help as we can get. I'm really thankful for people who pray for me. I should probably spend more time on my knees, but I've always been more of a doer than a pray-er. Fortunately, there's room for both in this world.

Now, I do have a bone to pick with some folks. I think that there is a big difference between what I call a "Shirtsleeves Christian" and a "Roll-Up-Your-Shirtsleeves Christian."

Shirtsleeves Christians are the kind of people who believe in wearing their Christianity on their shirtsleeves. A Shirtsleeves Christian is the kind of person who spends more time quoting chapter and verse than doing anything about the advice in that passage. A Shirtsleeves Christian worries more about how high the steeple is in his church, or how nice the seats are, than if people really pray there or if the church social room might be used to tutor underprivileged children. A Shirtsleeves Christian looks down at people of other faiths or even at people of other Christian denominations instead of respecting them and trying to work with them to solve our problems. Shirtsleeves Christians spend more time bellyaching about how immoral and godless the world is rather than making the world a more responsible and better place to live.

On the other hand, Roll-Up-Your-Shirtsleeves Christians try to get things done in the real world in a Christian way. They behave like Christians in the workplace and in school. They teach their children values and believe in caring discipline no matter what other parents may do. They support good causes. They dig into life and try to make things better for people who deserve a break.

Roll-Up-Your-Shirtsleeves Christians believe Christianity is faith *and* action. They still make the time to talk with God through prayer, study Scripture with devotion, be super-active in their church, and take their ministry to others to spread the Good Word. Those are people like Billy Graham and Mother Teresa, Pat Robertson and the late Norman Vincent Peale. And there are also thousands more of what my editor Lyn Cryderman calls "little guys and gals in the pew"—anonymous people who may be doing even more good than all the well-known Christians in the world. In my book, there's another name for Christians like that—saints. The Bible reminds us that "Many who are first shall be last; and the last shall be first."

Let me give it to you tongue-in-cheek: In the great hereafter I want the job rating I get for my life to show that I did some good while on this earth. In short, I want to be a better Roll-Up-Your-Shirtsleeves Christian in the years to come than I am today. And I'm working on it.

But back to heaven: there's no doubt in my mind that plenty of other folks have done much more good than I have, and many of them will be there, too. Of course, just doing good won't get you to heaven. If I get there, I'll probably have a place further down the table from those folks in the seating arrangement in the heavenly banquet hall. But that's okay, just as long as the Lord still lets me wear my shirtsleeves rolled up.

KEEPING CONVICTIONS CLEAR

Convictions aren't just religious beliefs. Conviction also means staying true to your principles—whether you're a single parent or in a business or community organization.

In my business, quality is probably the number-one conviction on our list. Some people will tell you that they have a great eye for quality and they're always willing to pay the price for it. When the quality is real, that's just great. Some people, though, get soaked paying for quality that isn't real, but which they think is real. In fact, while they believe they are discriminating consumers, they don't really know what they're doing. Let me give you some examples about quality from the food industry.

Ron Fay is a friend and colleague of mine who's made a real contribution to Wendy's. He understands quality like Ray Charles understands rhythm and blues. Ron can tell you about a group of restaurants that invested in an attempt to buy bigger french fries and forgot about *execution*, which is at the heart of delivering quality to customers. They had a wrong conviction and mistook paying more for a product as the end-all in delivering quality.

When Ron got into it, he found that the customer was getting lousy fries. The more expensive fries overloaded the baskets and caused improper cooking, and the fries weren't being seasoned properly, and consequently, ended up limp and soggy. Procedures like these caused the restaurants to pay more and deliver less quality. In fact, when they fixed the situation, they saved $55,000 a year!

As Ron tells people, "You can't just buy quality. It also includes how you execute at the store level. Sure, you have to buy fine ingredients, but you also have to focus on people skills in order for quality to prevail." I'm sure that as many hard-working students have gotten a quality education out of little Eureka College (Ronald Reagan was one of them) as have out of a prestigious place like Cambridge (which includes Soviet master spy Kim Philby among its graduates after he served for years in British intelligence). Expecting too much from better-than-thou ingredients is a big way that people screw up making quality decisions—and their convictions—about people, about food, about anything. A hefty price tag or a fancy reputation is no guarantee of an honest-to-goodness quality result.

Whether it's obtaining true quality in food products or really caring about people, faith in pursuing your mission is still what counts. It reminds me of an old story about Mother Teresa helping the poor in Calcutta. When an admirer came up to her and asked just how it was going to be possible to feed these millions of starving people, she answered that you have to do it just one mouth at a time.

The same is true for adoption. I believe that any campaign for adoption succeeds if just one youngster gets adopted as a result. If that happens, it all will have been worth it. Like Mother Teresa, if we think about people as individuals, it's a lot easier to find the quality inside of them—often hidden—than if we think about them as a group.

After quality, the next thing people seem ready to pay for is service. Certainly, friendly and courteous treatment should be a top priority. But you have to be able to deliver the goods, too. Some restaurants fake it. They lay on the gourmet and overdo the bows and scrapes. Maybe some people like that when they eat out, but I sure don't.

A fine example of a restaurant that combines quality food and quality service is Pete's in Boca Raton, Florida. Next to Wendy's, Pete's is my favorite restaurant. Pete Boinis serves the best prime rib and finest swordfish I've ever tasted. Every time I'm there, the dining room is full and the customers are smiling from ear to ear.

Some restaurants have a deserved reputation for service. If you want to be successful in buying quality or in delivering it, you deserve to know what allows that to happen. It isn't because the staff all gets together before dinnertime and the captain says, "OK, gang, let's get out there and serve." It's because a restaurant is what Ron Fay calls "rush ready." You put things in place before they need to be. You set an extra spatula on the grill before the rush so that a server can help out if a bigger-than-expected wave of customers hits.

How many times in history have you seen cases of supposed quality organizations that weren't "rush ready"? Was the government's Immigration and Naturalization Service "rush ready" for the wave of illegal aliens coming over our borders in the 1970s and 1980s?

Were the courts "rush ready" for the growing crime problem of recent years? Should they have had the "extra spatula" of temporary prisons in mind rather than letting dangerous criminals back out to prowl the streets while new prisons were being built? I think so. There are some mighty fine judges and court workers out there, but we often rate the quality of our legal system by how sophisticated its codes and laws are, and less often by the quality of the job it gets done.

And most of all, I think our faith has to be "rush ready." Ready to meet the challenges that our hectic and unpredictable world presents every day.

PINGO! IT'S POSITIVELY PAT

When people think of Pat Robertson, they think of achievements like the Heads Up literacy program, Regent University, the Christian Coalition, and his past presidency of the Council for National Policy. Great stuff. But one of my oldest memories of Pat is Pingo the Bear and Pingo's trip to the moon.

I was traveling in Virginia in the early- or mid-sixties when I saw a television show on the Christian Broadcasting Network (CBN), a cornerstone for so much of what Pat Robertson has achieved. These were the early days of CBN, and their studio was pretty simple—in fact, there was only one studio at the time. A regular feature was a kid's program starring a puppet called Pingo the Bear. On this particular show, the story line was to launch Pingo on a trip to the moon. Pingo sat on his little rocket. Then, *shaa-bamm!!!* Off it went.

Suddenly there was this big explosion and the screen went completely white—and seemed to be all covered with snow. Had the television set in the motel room lost the channel, I asked myself? I walked over to the old Muntz T.V. and started fidgeting with the rabbit ears—poking them in all different directions and pounding on the side of the box so that the coins in the timer on the side jingled like cymbals. (Yes, young-uns. That's what "pay T.V." meant back then.)

No improvement in the picture. Finally I could see this young guy, Cousin Neil—Pingo's sidekick—show up on the screen, walking through a gray, pea soup fog. So I knew that the problem wasn't the set in the room.

Cousin Neil was clutching a ukelele, but he wasn't singing. He gasped that Pingo had landed safely on the moon. Then the next show came on that same station, a music program. A chorus decked out in choir robes was singing hymns—at least they tried to sing; after the first brave notes the singers started sputtering and coughing to beat the band. "Onward, Christian cough-cough. . . ." I don't know how they made it through. Years later Pat told me that the special effects guy got a little smoke happy and, because they had just one studio, the choir ended up paying the price for Pingo's moon outing.

Since then I've been a guest on Pat's 700 Club and have seen the layout of CBN's studios today. I'll tell you this: I'm not sure Pingo could ever make it in the space age, but I do know that Pat Robertson has. Today CBN is the largest television ministry in the world—reaching 9,000 communities in the United States and fifty foreign countries. And all this from a guy who in 1959 rolled into Virginia from New York with his wife and three children at the wheel of a used DeSoto and a 5' x 7' U-Haul hitched behind him. He had 70 bucks to his name. He raised the $35 filing fee to start broadcasting through contributions and opened a bank account with three one-dollar bills. He's come a long way since those days. Talk about well done!

Wendy's is a national advertiser, and we're always on the lookout for the right settings for our ads. We have close ties to one particular Pat Robertson operation, and that's the Family Channel. An offshoot of CBN, the Family Channel was one of the first three cable networks to rent space on the first satellite transponder (the other two were Ted Turner and HBO). Until it had five million subscribers, the Family Channel had just one employee, then it expanded to two. Today the Family Channel has 55 million subscribers!

The Family Channel is a heck of a success story, and I think that it succeeds for one big reason: Pat Robertson had the conviction to find an audience that he knew others were deserting—an audience committed to basic values.

I believe that the *way* Pat Robertson's business grew was a big reason as to why he became so successful and how he was able to find such a neat niche in the marketplace. The three big television networks grew up in radio days. By the time the fifties had rolled around, they had grown from their local base to being large national firms. On the other hand, Pat's CBN— the cornerstone of the Family Network—was a collection of local UHF television stations that gradually built itself up market by market, first in Virginia, then in Atlanta, next in Dallas, and then in Boston. The first one had an itty-bitty one-kilowatt transmitter. Pat still likes to talk about how he would spend hours poring over the rating books to figure out how he could compete with the big three networks. He told it to me this way:

"I knew the rating of almost every show in almost every major market in America. We could tell you which programs flowed with which, and I would sit down with a big piece of paper and map it all out. It was like going to battle. I knew what the networks would put up against me. Then I would see what kind of team I could put on the field against them."

As the networks became more sensational and less mainstream in the values they showcased, Pat dropped his anchor in family fare—religious programming, Westerns, some sitcoms, cartoons, and children's programs. Years later, when I started Wendy's, my two biggest competitors were already big chains. I found my niche, too, and was able to grow.

Today, the Family Channel is riding the comeback wave in supporting wholesomeness and family values. People are fed up with crime, violence, and delinquency. I know that I'm not the first to say this, but the television set in most American homes today is what the fireplace or potbelly stove was for the generations before us—the focal point. If that means everybody's staring at pictures of murder and mayhem in living Technicolor and getting away with it, who is going to stick around home eating popcorn? Some people find their worst side start to tingle and want to get out there and in on the action themselves!

Now Pat has expanded into producing entertainment programs too—shows like *Big Brother Jake, Zorro, Bordertown,* and *Snowy River*. And it's kind of funny—but I kinda think great—that the networks are buying these shows up, because I really believe that they are seeing the errors of their ways. The big three put themselves so far out into left field with sensationalism that no self-respecting dish detergent, disposable diaper, or deodorant advertiser wants to be seen in the company of some of their shows.

What can Pat Robertson teach all of us about success coming from convictions? The first thing is that the biggest successes are usually built from the grass roots up. You start out with one restaurant, a little machine shop, or a one-person computer programming workshop in your attic. Or you can begin with winning over the trust of just one member of a cut-throat street gang, the loyalty of a single family in an immigrant community, or the confidence and respect of a hardened, cynical politician. Faith is built one person at a time. That's how you launch space satellites, cook hamburgers, or save souls. At Wendy's we serve one customer at a time. I try to get one child adopted at a time. One-by-one thinking is the first step to succeeding in a world that seems to be running out of control.

Second, study the numbers—and I mean really study them. Whenever the crowd stampedes in one direction, there are usually plenty of others who will either stay put or move in another direction. We make too big a deal, I think, out of fads and trends. To succeed, you may have to do battle inch-for-inch as Pat did with the big networks, but you can do it. That's what competition is all about. We would like the world to be run on a win-win basis, but a big part of our life is competition, too. The Oscars, the Heisman Trophy, the Fortune 500 ... even the Special Olympics and the Nobel Peace Prize are competitions.

Third, you have to be positive. Does it do a lot of good to go protesting against the newest shoot'em-out, slice'em-up, strip-it-off movie? Or is it better to make a show like *The Waltons* or *Big Brother Jake*? If the tide seems to be running against what you believe in, support what is right first and foremost, and second, support what is sensible.

Discipline

Routine is at the heart of discipline. Routine is what keeps us focused on the basic, main things in life. Routine doesn't have to mean boring. And unless you have a strong, healthy routine, I doubt that you can live a successful life. Discipline means keeping things and people in their proper places. For example, I think that taxpayers should discipline their politicians so that they don't get too uppity. Children need discipline, too—plenty more than most of them get—and that's more the fault of the parents than the kids. Discipline means direction—clear and firm direction—not physical or mental abuse. Discipline also helps you keep track of your own thinking and keeps it simple and to the point so that you don't mess up by dreaming up fancy, big-shot thoughts when you don't need to.

I've already mentioned Roy Tuggle and the role he played in developing Jim Near, Wendy's Chairman and CEO. Roy is a classic in discipline as far as I'm concerned. When he was fourteen years old, Roy—the sixth of twelve children—left Ravenna, Kentucky, during the Great Depression. With only two years of school under his belt, nine pennies in his pocket, and cardboard soles in his shoes, he hopped a freight train to Columbus, Ohio. After unloading stoves and refrigerators and working as a dishwasher, he became a fry-cook. By sheer will and discipline he built his career and a great restaurant business while he and his wife Mary raised their family.

When Roy started out, hamburgers were only a nickel and a small restaurant operator had to scrimp for every penny. Years later, when Roy sold his business, he became a millionaire. But the dollar signs never changed Roy. He's never been driven by money. As you'll hear Roy put it, "I never wanted to be the richest man in the graveyard," to which I'll generally chime in, "You got it Roy. You've never seen a hearse with luggage racks." As I see it, that's another type of discipline—the kind that keeps success from going to your head once you've had the good fortune to achieve your goals.

THE WONDER OF ROUTINE

Wendy's president Gordon Teter may be the most routine guy I've ever met, and I mean that as a compliment. He comes from a deeply religious family. At Purdue University, he was a great scholar, quite a football player, and a campus leader. Gordon's really smart. Even better, he has a strong streak of common sense. I think he can handle any job at Wendy's. One of the great things that Gordon taught us in running the Wendy's business was to keep it focused and keep it balanced.

For a while, Wendy's was what I would call promotion-crazy. One month we would promote our single hamburgers at 99¢ and the average restaurant would sell thousands of them. The next month we'd promote chicken sandwiches at a special price, and most of our restaurants would sell a couple thousand of those. All this commotion brought in tons of customers, so you would think that it was a great idea.

Honestly, it was a lousy idea, because a restaurant that sells thousands of hamburgers one month is a different restaurant from one that sells a thousand chicken sandwiches. Because of our advertising, we were basically changing what kind of restaurant we were every thirty days. That's what Gordon told us.

One of the things that made Wendy's a better restaurant was actually putting a limit on the number of good ideas that we had—or at least the number that we decided to *act on* at any one time. Instead of having fifty good ideas a month and doing them all hit-or-miss, we decided we would have only two or three good ideas and execute the heck out of them. We slowed ourselves down and learned our routine. A lot of people try to do and be everything—too many things—at once. Just do what you can and be who you are.

It's not easy to be disciplined, and that brings me back to Gordon Teter. Not because he's a Wendy's guy, but because he is who he is. Let's look a little bit closer at Gordon's background to see how he got such a knack for discipline.

Gordon's father, Fred, was an executive with the drug company Eli Lilly out of Indianapolis. Gordon's grandfather owned a farm, but it was really Gordon's father and his brother Jim who ran it. And Gordon, too. The farm was a good-sized operation with corn and soybeans, cows and pigs. Gordon pulled his weight on the farm, which meant tending to the animals at five in the morning and in the evening, too. It also spelled an extra push from everybody during planting and at harvest time.

Gordon's mother, Bonnie, was a substitute teacher. She came out of a foster home and really appreciated the value of a family and an education. So you can understand why Gordon hit the books as hard as he did. Gordon's home was steeped in strong Christian values.

This all explains a lot about Gordon. But where did he learn all this great stuff about disciplining yourself to keep things simple? Maybe it was when he was playing high-school football at Lawrence Central in the small town of Lawrence, Indiana. His team won a lot of games. What was their secret? Seventy-five percent of their offense was just four different plays. The other twenty-five percent were little "wrinkles" on those four plays. You don't have to out-fox people. Mostly, you just have to do the basics well, time and again.

Gordon did a lot as a kid, but he didn't try to do too many different things—just as his football team was disciplined and didn't try to do too many fancy maneuvers. I think that most American families are too busy trying to do too many good things for themselves and for their kids—ballet class, swimming team, soccer tryouts. No kid has to play five sports, and no parent has to belong to five church committees. When you take on that big a load, how much can you really do well? Can your life ever really follow a sensible routine—the kind of routine that lets you get things done well, day in and day out?

A lot of folks today don't like routine. Not me. I'm all for it. Take clean restaurants, for instance. If there ever was a routine that needed following it's getting a restaurant ready to open for customers every day. As I travel around the country visiting Wendy's restaurants, the managers always know I'm coming. Not surprisingly, a lot of extra effort goes on before I get there to make the restaurants sparkling clean. I'm glad they do it, but I wish I could get every manager to act like I was going to visit their restaurant every day of the year.

Routine can help in lots of other ways, too. It can cure the most unexpected things. Being short in the cash register is a problem in many restaurants. Sometimes it's internal theft. Often it's making change carelessly, especially when there are a lot of customers. Retailers and restaurants have all kinds of ways of fighting shorts in the register. Video cameras, surprise inspections, even undercover spies. But do you know what the single best weapon against register shortages is? None of the above. It's simply the discipline of routine reporting. Having people call in the shortages for their restaurant to the home office every day. The shortages could be low. They could be high. Whatever they are, you don't beat people up over the phone for what they report. But the simple fact that they have to report their shortages makes people pay more attention to what they're doing and helps keep a handle on the problem.

Families have routine disciplines. Or at least they should:

- Homework is a routine, and there should also be routine reporting of how things are going in the different classes.

- Chores are a routine, and the reporting about what got done and what didn't should be pretty clear.

- Church, praying, or spending some time with a sick or lonely relative—those are good routines.

- Eating together and talking a few nights a week is a good routine for a family to fall into. (Heck, what did you expect a restaurant guy to say?)

PART-TIME POLITICIANS AND CITIZEN CUSTOMERS

We really complain about our politicians. "Crooks and liars" we call some of them. Overall, I admire people who are truly dedicated to serving the public. But some politicians get away with murder because we—the taxpayers—don't discipline them. For one thing, we've let this crazy notion spring up that politics is always a full-time job. It may be for a mayor or governor, but it shouldn't be for legislators or members of Congress.

I really believe in part-timers. Quick-service restaurants couldn't survive without having a huge force of skilled, well-trained part-time workers. We need part-timers in restaurants, retail stores, and hundreds of other industries. But do you know where we need part-timers most of all? In government! We really need part-time officials to be elected to Congress, because if our legislators were out living by the rules they made, they wouldn't make so many laws, and the ones they did make wouldn't be so stupid so often. Think about it! Thomas Jefferson, John Adams, and their buddies had to make a buck to support themselves. They never intended Congress to be run by a bunch of professional bureaucrats and politicians.

All these positions we hear about in politics are important to know. But aren't there other skills and experiences that may be even more important? For example, if creating and preserving jobs for Americans is one of our biggest national issues, should we let people serve in Congress if they never had the discipline of doing a payroll? If we want smart investment decisions, should we have people sitting in Congress who never took out a business loan to open a plant or an office? Should we let people run our government who have never saved money or delivered quality products? The bottom line is this: We need to elect the most qualified people, not the ones who try to be the most popular.

This may sound like sacrilege, but sometimes when I think of that beautiful Capitol building in Washington, I think of it in terms of a Wendy's restaurant: Does the facility work? Do the people working there think of it as a place where they need to get a job done? Does it meet the needs it's supposed to?

A Wendy's is designed to feed people good food at fair prices every day with quick, efficient service. Shouldn't the Capitol in Washington be designed to deliver everyday people good laws with a fair price tag in a prompt way? Why not? Bottom line, shouldn't we be measuring government by its efficiency as well as its effectiveness? I think so.

One way that might work is to measure and rein in the size of congressional staffs. Why not tighten the square footage that can be used by each staff? How about putting regulators on the air conditioning and even the lights—making it less like a luxury hotel and more like where regular people work? The biggest single thing we could do to pick up the pace of federal government could be to install straight-back chairs throughout all of elected and appointed Washington. I'd do that in a heartbeat. It would shorten meetings and prevent politicians from thinking up zany new laws or going through foolhardy debates staged for T.V. cameras. The same goes for statehouses and city councils, too. (You may be chuckling, but if you don't have discipline about the simple things, you'll never have it about the tough ones.)

Congressman Dan Burton from Indianapolis is one sharp guy on Capitol Hill. He's one of the few members of Congress around (there are some other good ones, like John Kasich, but I want to single Dan out) who sincerely believes that we have to cut our deficit. Even when it comes around to budget time and incumbents go hell-bent for reelection by trying to protect every little pork-barrel project in their districts, Dan and a few others like him have the guts to stand up for what is right.

Dan thinks that the way to fix this problem is to put a cap on total government spending, then put the approval authority for specific projects in the hands of individual agencies rather than leave it in the control of Congress. This way local media and special interests would be less able to put the squeeze on individual members of Congress. Each year the Departments of Defense, Transportation, and so forth would decide how to spend their individual budgets. Congress would be responsible for setting the spending cap for each agency and tying the individual budgets together through the Ways and Means Committee.

Big corporations have had this kind of discipline for years. The CEO says to the heads of each of the divisions, "Here's what you have to work with. Spend it according to your plan." That's what delegation means. But not in government. Lately, it seems to me, instead of getting the promised budget decreases, we ended up getting budget increases.

Unless we can get a cap on spending and on the deficit, Dan Burton knows—and I agree with him—only one thing is going to happen: Inflation and prices will grow like crazy, and then we'll be sitting in the middle of another recession.

Let me add my two cents to Dan Burton's thoughts on Congress by pointing out a couple of other things that could help balance the federal budget. One would be to give the president a line-item veto to strike out unnecessary expenses in the the bills Congress approves. The second would be to limit congressional terms in office so we don't encourage career politicians. Changes like these could motivate politicians to do the right thing even when their decisions may not be popular and might cost them votes.

The other thing that Dan Burton worries about is what we're doing to the small businessperson. Medical insurance for everybody is a great idea, but we have to be careful about how we pay for it. If we throw too much of the burden on small businesspersons they will either cut back on their employees, raise their prices, or move their businesses out of the country. Maybe all three.

Taking Advantage Of Age

Discipline is as much for the older people as it is for young ones. Some of the disciplines I believe in aren't fancy, but they seem to work.

I first met Colonel Sanders of Kentucky Fried Chicken fame when he was sixty-five. He could be very charming, but he traveled a lot, riding around the country in his Cadillac, and I could see that he tired easily. As I grow older, the biggest thing I notice about succeeding at what I want to get done is that I get tired faster. Older people who are successful need to be able to *pace* themselves. My trick is to "batch" my time. Rather than trying to work eight hours at a stretch, I'll go in spurts of two or three hours. I also do the very best I can to steer clear of dumb work. No memos if I can just talk to someone on the phone. In fact, almost no memos at all.

Humor is important. To get people to listen, I often find that you have to get them to laugh a little first. I think that older people have a responsibility to teach and remind younger ones that life should be fun. If older people walk around complaining about *this* disease or *that* ungrateful child, everybody under sixty is bound to believe that life is a bummer, and that it only gets worse day by day. Keeping a good attitude is really a matter of discipline, and people are responsible for having their outlook on life as positive as it can be.

Walk a lot. No kidding. I walk all the time. Unless your doctor says you shouldn't, I think that walking is the healthiest way to work off a Frosty or a baked potato with cheese and bacon.

Meet new people. Some people think that the older they get, the fewer people they should know. I knew very few people as a kid. Today I know plenty more people at the age of sixty-two than I did at the age of fifty-two. That's the way it should be, don't you think? And most of those people aren't celebrities either, but folks working in the community.

Listen. I think that's a really big thing for older people.

Older people have a big reputation for *giving* advice. Is the advice we give really all that great? Maybe we would do better by just lending an ear and being supportive. We like to reminisce and tell war stories, and that's good, I guess. But it takes real discipline for an older person to be a supportive listener for a younger one. Try it some time.

BATTLE OF THE BILLS

Some people would rather go face-to-face with a dental drill than face up to the need for a personal budget. You can't avoid budgets. If you can't manage money, you won't be successful in life. You don't have to be rich or own your own company, but you have to be able to manage money. It's as simple as that. Maybe you're determined to live a modest life or even to stay poor. Well, there are dumb ways to live poor and smart ways to live poor. I know poor people who live in simple, clean little homes and raise large families on low wages—decent people who have values and raise their kids to believe in the right things. Nothing to be ashamed of there.

I also see aimless drifters—who are not disabled or mentally challenged—who are living on the street and making a mess out of their lives. The evening news shows us plenty of them every day. Smart poor people have budgets and respect money. Undisciplined, uneducated poor people are likely to squander the little bit that they have.

I may be a millionaire today, but thirty-two years ago, when we moved to Columbus, Ohio, and I was trying to turn around a group of failing chicken restaurants, we had nearly everything on payments. That included the house, the car, the T.V., the vacuum cleaner. Our whole life was $5 here and $3 there. (Lorraine tells me that she even thinks that our collie, Missy, was on payments, but I don't know about that.)

Lorraine still sewed most of the kids' clothes because we couldn't afford any better at the time. When we went to our first black-tie dinner, I rented a tux and Lorraine made her own dress. I remember putting aside quarters and dimes to buy a new living room sofa. Today, I still live with budgets at Wendy's every day. We may be a $4 billion company going on $5 billion, but we seem to have a budget for everything.

A budget is both a plan and a scorecard. Many—maybe most—people do a bad job of budgeting. I think it's because they make it too complicated and waver between being too soft and too hard on themselves. I've been told that money problems are still the single biggest reason that marriages and families break up.

CBS television has a regular on *CBS This Morning* whose name is John Stehr. A while back, John offered to send viewers a little planning sheet for family finances called "John Stehr's MoneyWise Budget Guide." It has a family spending plan, lists of things people spend their money on, and it gives tips on how to spend less. Real simple.

Well, I was curious. I called John up and asked him how many people wrote in for this little sheet. John had been floored by the response. Sixty thousand people had written in for this guide. People are dying for some common-sense advice about how to manage the family budget.

John is my version of common sense on two feet, and he has some solid advice for families who have had a tough time managing their budgets. The way to start thinking about a budget is to figure out what you have to spend every month ("fixed" expenses) and what aren't absolute musts.

The second step is to make what John calls the "leap of faith." That means that you have to really believe that you are responsible and accountable for managing your money.

Most people don't understand credit cards at all. Credit cards can be the most dangerous threat to successfully managing a family's money. Many people buy things that aren't really necessary on credit—things like vacations, fancy clothes, sporting equipment. These are things people could do without, and the credit bills build up. Before you know it, one of the biggest fixed expenses that a family has each month is paying on their credit bills.

John also pointed something out to me that knocked my socks off: Credit card interest charges are so high that a person can actually pay for an item three or four times by stretching out the payments on credit. Three or four times! A $50 lamp can end up costing $150 or $200; a $400 airplane ticket can put you out over $1,000. And usually all that money could be saved or used elsewhere if you just wait and save in the first place.

When I suggested to John that balancing a budget is a lot like losing weight, he agreed. The biggest problem that people have losing weight—I think—is that they try to do too much, make their goals too hard, get frustrated, and then jump off of the diet. Just like you have to climb on a scale every day or two, you also have to look at where your finances stand pretty regularly. It has to be part of everybody's goals for living successfully. It may be just a part, but it has to at least be part of your goals, or you are headed for one miserable life. And you have to be realistic, too. Not everybody is perfect in everything. I can still manage a budget—looking at my own personal case—better than I can manage a waistline. I have been on every diet known to man, and they haven't seemed to make a dent—so I have to assume my figure is God-given. (He sure was generous with me, wasn't he?)

My other budget Einstein is John Casey. John is Wendy's vice chairman of finance. He's Mr. Budget-in-Business, as far as I'm concerned. John uses a word that I really like as far as budgets are concerned. The word is "prudence."

John says that prudence involves choices. As John puts it, smart people make smart choices. They look at all the facts and alternatives when they buy a refrigerator, a car, or even a college education. They pick out the relevant information and focus on it:

- For a refrigerator, the energy it uses is more important than some special gizmo of a chiller to keep your radishes crisp.

- For a car, the trade-in value for the make is much more important than styling gimmicks.

- For a college education, the success that graduates of a particular school have in getting a job is one measure prospective students should consider.

John Casey also has one other tip for family success in handling the budget: Don't make a commitment you can't live up to. That's just another way to say: Be prudent.

Budgets are not a fun part of life. There just isn't much I can say about them that's inspirational. You have to live with them, that's all. If you think living with budgets is a headache, I can only guarantee you that living without them is plenty worse for you and the people you love.

I once heard of a budget "trick" that makes a lot of sense. Plenty of people get paid every two weeks. That means they get their paycheck twenty-six times a year. What if you budget yourself so that you cover all of your expenses with two paychecks each month (twenty-four per year)? But twice each year you get three paychecks in a month. These "extra" paychecks can now be used for Christmas money, vacation money, or gravy for the kids' college education account. It doesn't work for everybody, but this technique has really helped a lot of people, I hear.

And let's not forget the kids. Teaching kids to manage money is one of the best ways to teach them responsibility. It makes my blood boil sometimes when I hear people talk about youngsters getting their first job and working for minimum wage. These know-it-all adults talk about minimum wage as if it were beneath people's dignity, rather than building kids up and showing them the opportunity they have. I started my career before minimum wage laws even existed. I know a lot of people with more talent and education than I have who started at minimum wage and who are now very successful entrepreneurs or executives or community leaders. They have told me that their first job taught them plenty about getting along with people, understanding customers, and learning a lot of other things that go into responsibility.

Allowances are another good way of teaching responsibility if they are given to kids in the right way. I have a friend, Ron Scherer (a great father, I might add), who is well-to-do and who has paid his kids a fifteen-dollar allowance each week for a pretty long time. That's a big allowance, but Dad has some catches in his pay plan. Five dollars goes for spending money. Five dollars goes into a savings account, to be used for a big item like a tennis racket or a CD player—but only with Dad's approval, and five dollars is tucked away for college.

Pretty good plan, I think. And if the kids feel that they're paying for college (or a good chunk of it), how much harder do you think they'll study once they finally get there? Oh, by the way, at report card time, the five dollars of spending money is docked one buck for every grade below a B. If this Dad were teaching budgeting in a big-time business school, I don't think that nearly as many savings and loan associations would have gone belly-up. Do you?

NEVER ENOUGH

One day I was strolling through the Mercato Mediterranean Village—a shopping mall near Orlando. Gussied up in my red-and-blue Wendy's jacket and Wendy's baseball cap, I was just hanging out, practicing my Bill Cosby walk and other moves my grandchildren have tried to teach me. Suddenly this tall, tanned, athletic guy in a plaid shirt and beige slacks streaks by me. He's good looking, middle-aged. The silver-rimmed sunglasses focus my eyes on his high, Dwight Eisenhower-sized forehead. *He's probably got a brain and a half in there*, I say to myself. I'm curious because I think I recognize him.

He dashes into a Mexican restaurant called José O'Day's and slaps together a couple of tacos at the buffet. As I watch through the open doorway, he sits down at a table with a bunch of electronic gear in back of it, and a waiter brings him a glass of orange juice. Just then, an announcer booms out that this is Sports Radio 540 and that the next phone interview guest will be Dave Checketts, president of the New York Knicks. The Thin Man has dropped his shades and whipped on a headset. He and Dave Checketts are having a very smooth, very sharp back-and-forth about big-league basketball. Sure, I know this talk show host: It's Pat Williams, general manager of the Orlando Magic, and what I'm seeing is his regular weekly talk show.

You cannot be out there working on the adoption cause and not have heard of Pat and his wife, Jill. They are legends. All told, they have eighteen children. Four are birth children; fourteen are adopted, but—as Pat will tell you—he can't remember which of the eighteen are adopted. They've written about the crisis their marriage hit in its tenth year in a wonderful book called *Rekindled*. Back then they had three biological kids, but somehow this wasn't enough. When Jill Williams grew up in the Chicago suburb of Riverside, she played with dolls, running an orphanage in her mind's eye. The dolls never looked like her, but she was the mother and in charge of them.

Today Jill's dream is reality, and—believe me—it is taken seriously. Among the adopted children are South Koreans, Brazilians, Romanians, and four brothers from the Philippines. There are seven thirteen-year-olds in the family.[1] This demands big-league family management. Pat will tell you that he knows some people consider this to be a "frantic accumula-

---

1. For more interesting background on the Williams family I recommend an excellent article by Jack McCallum called "Family Matters," *Sports Illustrated*, April 21, 1993, 32f.

tion of children" and that these critics think it's "abnormal." But Pat and Jill are answering a call—or a calling. "God," Pat says, "has laid a burden on our hearts and equipped us with the financial means, the desire, and the good health to do it."

Who are Pat and Jill really doing this for? There's no doubt that it's for the children who would never have had a chance like this in their homelands, but I think it's also for the benefit of the rest of us. When the Williamses found that their own core family wasn't enough, they started to adopt. What I think is even more amazing is how the idea of "never enough" helps them parent. Pat and Jill Williams may have a special message for us all about what it means to be a successful parent, as hard as it is to be a father or mother today.

The Williams' household is strong on discipline and on love—a lot stronger on both of these than nearly any home I can imagine. Kids come to them out of total poverty. If you've survived the streets until you are five years old in places like Brazil and the Philippines and have come out alive, you are hardened, hardened with a crust that most adults in the United States will never know. You are used to begging—sometimes even stealing—just to stay alive. The Williamses see their job as breaking the will of the street without breaking the spirit of the child.

Their discipline is tough. Children are prodded to compete in athletics. Williams kids who could barely tread water have turned into swimming champions. Most of the kids pick up English at supersonic speeds, and teachers welcome them into their classrooms. In the main, the kids are A and B students, and when the kids reach the schoolroom they already know what discipline means. Outside of an occasional video, there's no television at home. Phone calls are limited. Jill figured it out: If each of the kids called two friends for ten minutes each night, it would take six hours to make it through all the kids. On the other hand, the Williams' home has a 7,000 book library. Bedtime is 9 P.M. for the older children, 7 P.M. for the younger ones, but the kids keep such a busy day that their heads hit the pillows tired.

Kids are assigned numbers. No way you could manage the laundry differently. A black board lists the names and numbers of those who miss chores or break the rules. What about punishment? Some of the kids react to a look; some need a time-out. Others may have to be reminded on the hand or the bottom. But there is absolutely no abuse. Jill says that women will come up to her after she makes one of her speeches and remark, "I've got a seven-year-old boy, and I simply can't control him." To which she will ask as an answer, "You are bigger than he is, aren't you?"

Pat gives the credit for the smooth running of the household to Jill, and he really sums up the heart of discipline when he says this about her, "The rules are the same from one day to the next. Jill does not wink." Jill's also not afraid to tell parents who are having a tough time juggling their schedules around three children to get a couple more, and the family's time is sure to be better managed.

Unconditional love and clear discipline are hallmarks of the Williams' home. People who meet the kids are surprised by how normal the young people are. They may have a spat from time to time, but they will as often help each other tie shoes or brush hair as not.

And there's one other ingredient to the Williams philosophy. Pat calls it second milers. When another chore needs doing or an errand has to be run or a spill must be cleaned up, Pat puts out an all-points bulletin in the Williams' home: "I'm looking for second milers." Usually he finds them.

We—as a people and as parents—have gotten soft and comfortable about raising families, and I'm no exception. How many of us have tried as hard at the job of being parents as Pat and Jill Williams do? Maybe they're trying to tell us something. Maybe we have to try harder. Maybe we have to put up with less back talk or laziness. Maybe we say the word "enough" to ourselves and to our children too soon. How much of a difference would it make if we were all just a little more disciplined, just a tad more determined to set examples ourselves—examples that our children might remember?

PART TWO

OUTWARD: TREATING PEOPLE RIGHT

Success may start inside, but it doesn't mean anything until you draw other people into the picture. The key is whether you are going to be fair to other folks—will you treat people right?

If you are to treat people right, you have to master three fundamentals: caring, teamwork, and support. Most of us are lucky enough to learn these basic ideas from our parents and should be pros at them by the time we're in nursery school. But I've met some Ph.D.s and millionaires who never seemed to have learned the words or have forgotten what they mean, and I bet that you know people like that, too. Not taking people for granted is a great way to steer a straight course outward and to do right by your fellow human beings.

Caring

Caring is the rock that has to be there before love is possible. Caring is feeling what another person feels. Some people call it empathy.

Genuinely caring about people usually leads to success. And really successful people widen the circle of people they care about more and more as they grow older.

Mary Kay Ash of Mary Kay Cosmetics once told me something I'll never forget. She said the one suggestion she got in life that helped her most was to "pretend that every single person you meet has a sign around his or her neck that says, 'Make me feel important.'"

Why aren't we just nice to people? Just before Christmas one year, I went to a Wendy's restaurant in Albuquerque to film a T.V. adoption segment with two youngsters. The little girl, who was about seven, had a fresh scar where her father had walloped her with a beer bottle. That scar wasn't going away. As we ate lunch, the girl and her older brother, who was about nine, finally started to look me and an old friend who was with me in the eyes, and that was none too easy for them. We talked about how important it was to stick together when you don't have other family. And then the boy said something I'll never forget: "I don't want to be adopted with her. Just look at her ugly scar!"

It may seem cruel, but he was right. The boy knew his sister's appearance would turn off many possible adoptive parents. And before you condemn him, think back for a minute: Were you any less selfish than that when you were nine? I doubt that I was.

My friend—who is kind of smart in a low-key way and who made it big-time building a big business over the years—reached into his wallet and pulled out two crisp one-hundred dollar bills. "You kids," he said in a real quiet voice, "don't have any money to buy Christmas presents. It's plain to see that. So I want you to buy some Christmas presents, but there's a catch. You can't buy anything for yourself. Think hard about what your brother or sister might like or need and buy that instead. Finally, you gotta write me a letter about what you got each other." That five-minute course in caring outdid the best universities anywhere. The kids made up. In January my friend received a letter about what they bought each other, and he sent a copy to me. The kids got adopted. As I hear it, they're quite a team, and their new parents are proud to have them—because of the way that they care for each other and for lots of other reasons, too.

FROM KILLERS TO KINDLY PEOPLE

If you go to Mary Previte's office at the Camden County Youth Center in Blackwood, New Jersey, you'll see a wall of pictures called The Story Wall. They're drawings from children the Center has had in custody over the years. These drawings aren't suitable for Winnie the Pooh. As Mary puts it, the Youth Center is no place for cream puffs.

The bright blue, green, and yellow walls mislead you. As does the lack of bars. The Center is a transit point for youthful offenders headed for trial in the criminal justice system. There are thirty-seven beds in the Center. Usually, they're all full. At one time last year, eight of those beds were slept in by kids there for murder. Some of these youngsters come from street gangs; some are former killer drug runners.

What does Mary Previte try to do with these kids? She makes sure that they have a full school day and a solid recreation program. She does anything and everything she can to boost their self-confidence. Every day she runs a clean-and-tidy inspection, checking under the bed for "dust fluffies." When things look good, she posts a smiley-face sticker on the door. Arsonists and hit men ("hit kids" I guess is more the truth), making sure that there are no dust balls under their beds? Believe it!

Mary gets it done—because she's tough. I mean tough. The daughter of missionaries, she spent three years in a Japanese prison camp in China during World War II.

I asked Mary what was the biggest turnaround that she had ever seen in twenty years of running the Center. She told me about a youngster I'll call Saleed. Saleed's dad was doing time, and his mother was a junkie. Saleed raised himself eating scraps out of dumpsters. Then he got adopted. Did he ever. He was "fathered" by the North 24th Street Black Possé, one of the toughest drug gangs in Camden. When he arrived at the Center he was as defiant and mean as they come.

One evening while Saleed was at the Center, the parents of a well-off, chubby, spoiled ten-year-old brought the youngster in to have him "scared straight" by seeing what would happen to him if he didn't stop acting up. So they put him in with these young toughs, and they started right in frightening the pants off him and loving every minute of it.

Then something happened that nobody expected. Saleed turned on a dime. He became what Mary says the black community calls "an old head." He told the others, "It ain't right to be scared this way." Saleed—who had been neglected and abused his entire life—quietly told the little brat, who had probably had everything he ever wanted, that he should stay in school and stay in line. How about that? The-kid-the-gangs-raised trying to steer the rich kid away from the world of trouble.

Mary has loads of stories like that one, and you can read them in a book she's written called *Hungry Ghosts*.[1] The story of Saleed is a classic. We all can learn from Mary's caring mission of building positive self-confidence in kids. Helping others helps your own self-esteem, too.

We've learned that on a corporate level: We have a lot of handicapped people who work for Wendy's. Some of them have Down's Syndrome or serious learning disabilities. Many have been told that they have been helpless all of their life and that God has decided that they are going to stay that way. We try to work with these young people and go the extra mile to build their skills and self-confidence. They almost always end up among the best employees. If they see that a baby seat has to be set up for a customer who has her arms full with a small child or if they spot a senior citizen having trouble managing a tray, these special employees will be among the first to help.

In most ways, these very special, gentle people couldn't be more different from the tough customers with whom Mary Previte has to deal. But isn't it strange—and wonderful—how

1. Mary Taylor Previte, *Hungry Ghosts* (Grand Rapids: Zondervan, 1994).

most everybody will come alive when given a real chance and enough self-respect to care about others?

THE MOST INTENSIVE CARE YOU CAN GET

Every family has had to deal with awful sickness. Isn't it a shame that it often takes dark days to bring us all together? My family joined forces the first time our clan faced serious illness. Unfortunately, I was unconscious when most of it happened—so I missed out on seeing all the Thomases pull together to comfort each other.

In June 1990, I got really sick. Colds, flu, even intestinal flu had never really bothered me over my lifetime. But, boy, was I feeling bad. Constant nausea. Vomiting. The whole thing came on suddenly, just before a big company meeting we had in Chicago. My daughter Wendy was taking part in the presentation. She had never known me to be really ill. BS & BI was my motto: Be Sturdy and Button-It-Up. Not this time. Finally, I knew I just couldn't go on and show up at the presentation, let alone talk or even look halfway decent.

I took a plane back to Columbus and had a talk with my family physician, Dr. Manny Tzagournis. The doctor admitted me into Ohio State University hospital immediately and started tests right away. Then things began to snowball. For practical purposes, I was alone. Lorraine was traveling in Italy with my daughters Pam and Lori and my daughter-in-law Kathy. My son Kenny and I were going through a rough stretch and weren't really talking with each other very much. Daughter Molly was in a remote little town in northern Michigan.

When Wendy heard I was in the hospital, she flew straight to Columbus. I told her not to come, that I could manage on my own. Luckily, she didn't listen to me. The doctors wanted to operate, and they needed authorization. I told Wendy that Lorraine, Pam, Lori, and Kathy should stay put in Florence, but she wouldn't listen to me. She said the family had to be together. I can still remember her pacing on the linoleum floor with a hand-held cellular phone in the corridor outside my room trying to "Buona sera!" her way through the Italian switchboards to get in touch with Lorraine. It was already the middle of the night there. Wendy talked with Molly, and Molly managed to charter a little puddle-jumper of a plane to get down to Columbus. Wendy also talked with Kenny, who headed down to the hospital.

While this was all going on, Wendy was the organizer. She and her husband Paul were expecting their first child and she was in her eighth month. She spent some "quality time" with dear old dad telling him that it was going to be okay and that it was just a question of having the right mental attitude. But dear old dad was scared to death—frightened about what the doctors were going to do to him. The surgeons decided to operate that evening.

Wendy and Molly were there as they were starting to put me under. Kenny arrived just as they wheeled me down to the operating room. I grabbed his hand and said, "Glad you're here, my boy." It was then that the doctors told the family that they couldn't rule out that cancer might be causing my nausea and vomiting.

The operation took nearly four hours. Thank God, they removed a benign tumor between my large intestine and my liver. I've not had a problem since. When they finally got me to the recovery room and intensive care, my kids said that I looked like a pathetic mess. Everybody wanted to baby me, but Pam was probably the coolest head. "See you around, Pop, when you're feeling better" was the way she felt.

I learned some lessons from the whole experience: That Wendy was right to bring the family together. That the family was right to come together and to share in making a big decision (it made us stronger and helped heal a few people-to-people wounds). And that cancer research is a pretty good area to support charitably.

The new cancer research hospital—that so many of us in Columbus had given generously to—opened two weeks to the day after they placed the last suture in me during surgery. The doctors did a great job in the old place where they worked, but I will never forget hobbling down to the dedication of the new facility, holding my stitches so they wouldn't burst, admiring the new building and thinking to myself, "Buddy, just how do you get yourself into these things?"

I've been a long-time contributor to causes like cancer research—especially the Arthur James Cancer Research Institute at Ohio State University in Columbus. Why? Because they say cancer can be licked with enough time, money, and effort. Good enough reason for me.

FAMILY BUILDERS BEAT WRECKING BALL

We have short memories. Millions of people have lost their lives for this country and the values it represents. People my age may be blessed with a clearer idea of leadership than some younger generations because we grew up during the era of great generals in World War II. We had role models like Douglas MacArthur, Dwight Eisenhower, and especially George Patton. I can still remember "Old Blood and Guts" pushing across France and Germany to the borders of Czechoslovakia as the European campaign ended. Patton was a hard worker with real discipline. He once wrote in a letter: "A pint of sweat will save a gallon of blood."[2]

Sweat is precious, I think, in war and in peace. I know of a neat program called the Family Builders, and there are a couple of reasons I like it. First, it's not fancy, and it's not even dramatic. But it's like General Patton's philosophy: Better a pint of sweat than a gallon of blood. It's the better way to show that you care. Family Builders gets involved in family situations

---

2. George Patton, *War As I Knew It* (New York: Houghton-Mifflin, 1947).

that are bordering on abuse. Let me tell you about one case involving a couple I'll call Gary and Kim.

Gary, a young man in his early twenties, was discharged from the army three thousand miles from his home. Gary was married with two toddlers, and his wife, Kim, was pregnant with a third child. They lived in a dreary, beat-up trailer. Gary tried but couldn't find a job, and he needed knee surgery. At night the couple slept on the couch so that the children could have the bed.

Neighbors reported the couple for child neglect. Come on! They weren't neglecting their children. This young couple was just poor! Family Builders got wind of the situation and they went to work. They found Gary a job, arranged for prenatal care for Kim, and moved the family into a subsidized apartment that cost them only $88 a month.

That's what a social worker would call a volatile situation. No telling what would have happened in Gary's or Kim's circumstances, but I can tell you what happens in too many cases like this: (1) the father throws up his hands and abandons the family, (2) the couple will take off for a bar and leave the children unsupervised, and/or (3) hatred and frustration take over in the home. The listening stops. The hitting starts.

You can get involved on the front end, caring about people the Family Builder way—or get involved later through the costs of civil case workers, welfare payments, law enforcement, state-run foster homes, and prisons. Take your pick.

RECYCLING—SPIRITUAL AND OTHERWISE

What a smile Mattie Hart has. Mattie Hart is one of my very favorite people in the whole world. After she and her husband, Sylvester, raised their own five children, they turned around and adopted *eleven more* children just to give them a home. I first met Mattie when she received the 1985 Child Advocate of the Year from the Children's Home Society of

Florida. Mattie drives a school bus and her husband works at a correctional institution. Under her loving care and home cooking, she has turned children with learning difficulties into honor-roll students and kids with growth disorders into football players and weight-lifters. This year, she'll have her second adopted child college bound.

Mattie is a real activist in the best sense of the word. She has a reputation for motivating churches in the community to tackle difficult adoption cases. One of her biological children has adopted three other youngsters. Mattie Hart isn't going to let any youngster she can help be tossed onto the garbage heap. No way!

I have met hundreds of foster children over the years, and many won't look you in the eyes. They're afraid to trust adults. When I looked into the eyes of Mattie's children, my heart jumped. I could see the love and self-confidence in each of her kids' faces. Mattie put that love and self-confidence there. That's how I measure success. Well done, Mattie Hart!

People talk a lot about recycling today. The greatest recycling in the world is when you give people back their opportunity. Sometimes that's done by helping people directly. Other times, it's recycling things that people who need a break can use. I have always liked stories about recyclers who do good, especially when they do lots of it. When I was in the service, I made quite a name for myself as an enlisted man who rummaged around trash that other units in our command were discarding. I wasn't ashamed to do it, because I often scrounged up utensils and other supplies that were just being wasted. In fact, it was often the same stuff that we were trying to requisition, but in the wacky world of the army what was scarce in one company was excess garbage in another.

So, when I looked through former President Bush's list of a "Thousand Points of Light"—a thousand people or groups in this country who are trying to do good things to help people out—I really took to the story of Justin Lebo.

Back in 1990, when he got his award, Justin was only thirteen years old. But even before then, when he was just ten, Justin found the basic parts of a beaten-up bicycle in the trash of a Saddle Brook, New Jersey, neighborhood. He rebuilt it for himself into a "Super Bike." His friends thought it was so good, he got a reputation for his skill. Then he made it his mission to redo old or discarded bikes for poor kids who couldn't afford them. To buy the parts he needed, he ran a lemonade stand and chipped in his allowance. Neat guy. In all, Justin rebuilt about 250 bicycles for poor kids.

Justin is seventeen now, has his driver's license, and is looking forward to college. He no longer recycles cycles, but he might do another project like his "bike-a-thon" some day. When you talk with Justin, it's pretty clear that he likes to do things that are clearly focused. What did Justin get out of what he did? The knowledge of "how extremely lucky I am," he says. That awareness can wake up caring in us humans—again and again.

"Bear" is fifteen years old—two years younger than Justin Lebo. His big brown eyes and blond hair melt almost any girl's heart. Bear can wiggle and jerk his bottom better than Elvis ever could.

When you walk by Bear, he goes into action. Thump-thump-thump. Sounds like a baseball bat whacking a broadloom carpet. And that's pretty close to what it is. Bear's tail is a good ten inches long and is in constant action pounding against the entryway floor he guards. Bear is a golden Labrador retriever, and he spends most of his time stretched out on his side by the door to the St. Jude's Ranch for Children on the shores of Lake Mead and in the shadow of Boulder City, Nevada.

Bear greets everyone who goes by. As I reckoned, old friends get three thumps; new friends get two. Kids have the place of honor: they generally get four. Sometimes Bear gets up, stretches, and wanders outside. Last week he spotted a prairie dog not far from the porch and nearly forgot his age. Hot pursuit in slow motion—willing spirit, weak legs.

The garden not far from the porch is where another piece of St. Jude's lore occurred about fifteen years ago, when Anglican nuns were still tending to the Ranch. Father Ward, the Anglican priest who runs the place, and Sister Rosamond were having a friendly little argument about this strange plant that was budding all over the garden. He said it was asparagus. She said it was sunflowers. It turned out to be wild marijuana! When they figured it out, priest and nuns pitched in for the fastest weed-trashing party in the history of the Nevada Territory.

St. Jude's is a refuge for mentally, physically, and sexually abused children. It's really a recycling center in every best sense of the word. It recycles greeting cards—I'll tell you about that in a minute—but most of all it recycles young lives that would otherwise be on the road to a very grim future. St. Jude's Ranch has nothing to do with St. Jude's Hospital. They're both great causes and share the same saint, but that's okay—St. Jude himself had a lot of versatility, as I hear it. It's a little hard to imagine that this ranch is about forty minutes from what many people think of as the "Sin City" of Las Vegas. In fact, the casinos give generously to St. Jude's Ranch. Plenty of people who live in Vegas grew up the hard way themselves, and they know about tough childhoods.

Father Herbert Ward—the spirit behind St. Jude—hails from Mississippi. He has a round face, rosy cheeks, and big, smiling eyes. That garden plot was really important to him. He couldn't find okra in the local stores. Without okra, he couldn't cook gumbo for his kids.

Father Ward's office walls are covered with photos of kids. There is a brigade of religious statues—all gifts that people have sent him—next to the personal computer on his desk. On the bookcase, between Bibles printed in Hebrew, Greek, and I don't know what all else, is a sign that reads "RELAX—God is in charge." Nice thought.

About forty-two kids live on the Nevada campus of St. Jude's. They all go to public school, and they all work on the ranch after school. Most of them work in the recycling center that takes the fronts of old greeting cards, pastes them up on a new backing, and packages them to send to people who donate money for the cards.[3] For their work, the kids are paid in scrip, a kind of ranch-only "currency."

The kids even buy their own toothpaste and shampoo with the "money" they earn. Father Ward found out that kids ended up in fewer toothpaste fights if they had to pay for stuff like that out of their own pockets. Every Friday the payroll is dished out to the kids at a place on the ranch called Jacob's Well.

Father Ward and his staff practice tough love—which I guess you could call caring to help what went wrong in a young person's life. Some of the youngsters are products of our country's wrong-headed welfare system. I think our welfare system should be as clear and as strict as Father Ward's work rules. Let me tell you how Father Ward deals with "entitlement outbreaks" that happen from time to time on the ranch. One ten-year-old I'll call Tony decided that he really didn't want to work. He said that work was dumb, and it didn't matter if he worked or didn't, that he'd get by. Father Ward decided that Tony really didn't need to get paid and he would also lose his shopping rights at the ranch store.

This went on for about three weeks. Tony then gave in and said that he wanted to go back to work. Father Ward said it wasn't going to be that easy. He wasn't sure that there were any more openings. Tony would have to write an application for the job. Then he'd have to go before a hiring committee. This all took time. Tony got his job back in the end. What a

---

3. You can help the St. Jude's Ranch; if you want to buy these special recycled greeting cards or have some old cards you'd like to send, the address of St. Jude's Ranch is 100 St. Jude's Street, P.O. Box 60100, Boulder City, NV 89006–0100.

worker he's been ever since! He'll probably be a hard worker for life because of the lesson he's learned.

Because of the shortage of nuns, lay people replaced them as staff members in the early 1980s. Nola Helm is a registered nurse and Father Ward's right-hand person. She grew up in Bowman, North Dakota, and she'll tell you that kids are tougher today than when she grew up. They may not have had it tougher in terms of luxuries, but they've seen it tougher in the realities they're exposed to. No surprise when you consider that "drive-by" murders can be seen on every T.V. screen and on too many neighborhood streets. Nola says that the ranch is now caring for the first generation of children abused by satanic loonies and occultists.

On the board of St. Jude's are an orthodontist and plastic surgeon who donate their services to repair some of the damage nature—and all too often—adults have done to these kids. A set of even teeth and a straightened nose can do a lot for a kid's self-image. One young fellow who had been pounded with a bottle by his father for moving some papers on a table told Father Ward that he was the lucky one. He reported that his little brother—officially listed as falling out of a cradle—was "smeared over the kitchen wall."

St. Jude's second campus is in Bulverde, Texas, and is home to twenty-four children. They've also launched a third campus in Big Spring, Texas. It's hard to imagine the saint in charge of impossible causes wearing a Stetson hat, but who ever expected that holy man to be in the recycling business, either?

Is there someone in your church or neighborhood that you could help "recycle" by giving them an odd job or by offering them an old living room set you were going to haul down to the community dump? Is there a run-down old building that could make a perfect youth center if people just donated some patience, paint, and perspiration? Recycling spells "care" in so many ways; it's just plain good for the heart and soul to do it.

CARING ISN'T BLACK AND WHITE

One of my main emphases in this book is on values that we hold ourselves as adults and those we teach our kids. Life presents an ongoing opportunity to learn and evaluate what our core beliefs really are.

I don't buy the idea that you get values once and for all when you're a kid. You can't vaccinate a kid against evil or doing bad things as if you were taking them to the doctor and giving them a shot against measles. No matter how strong the medicine, no matter how big the dose, values grow with people and vice versa. The most important thing that parents can do is to set the foundation for values.

I once asked Father Malloy, the president of Notre Dame and one of the brightest of the bright, about values. At the time, I was reading about all these colleges setting up departments and even entire centers for the study of business ethics. *Does this really work?* I wondered, and a lot of other businesses people have asked the same question. Can you start teaching a twenty-year-old college student all the things he or she *should* have learned about the time they first learned to brush their own teeth? Father Malloy answered that the biggest job of colleges should be to "be more critical about values already learned." Put Father Malloy's point about smartening up your values into practice.

A lot of values that we "learn" are just prejudices and signals that we pick up. But not all values are learned by rote at our parents' knee. The schoolyard teaches values; so does the street corner.

"Retarded people are strange."

"Uneducated people are lousy."

"Divorced people are immoral."

These bigoted views are rarely said as nicely as I've put them here, and the list goes on to include ugly slurs about people's race or religion.

The heroic San Francisco Giant pitcher Dave Dravecky, who almost made a playing comeback after cancer hit him but then lost an arm to the disease, has said some interesting things about how the whole experience affected him: "I used to see everything in black and white; now I see shades of gray in between. I used to think there was an answer for everything; now I realize many questions don't have answers."[4]

You have to build a basis for values. You have to let age and experience make those values wiser. And you have to hope that really knowing we aren't going to be around forever on this planet will make our values more humane.

Maybe children teach us the hardest lessons about death and life's values. Let me ask you a tough question: For little kids who are maybe two or three years old and suffering and almost sure to die in childhood, what are their values in life? How should they define success? What will have made their life a success?

Oh, I believe that they know when they are a success. Love is success. They know when they're getting it. You can see it in their eyes. When they're not, you can hear it in their cries.

Among those recognized by the Children's Home Society of Florida in 1994 were James and Charlene White. Since 1988 the Whites have been foster parents to babies born to HIV-positive mothers. In the six years since, the Whites have cared for over one hundred such kids and adopted four of them. Two of the adopted youngsters currently test negative; two others suffer from full-blown AIDS.

The Whites have founded a pediatric AIDS foundation called Serenity House for AIDS babies. So many parents dream of their children growing up to be movie stars or college professors, basketball pros or surgeons. The Whites have a different dream. They want to build a care center on ten acres of land to handle as many stricken babies as possible. President

---

4. Dave and Jan Dravecky with Ken Gire, "My Finest Hour," Reader's Digest, Oct. 1992, pp. 89–92. Adapted from *When You Can't Come Back* (Grand Rapids: Zondervan, 1992).

George Bush named the Whites one of the Thousand Points of Light in our country. The way the Whites see it, they are there to serve tragically infected children.

Well done, Charlene and James White, for what you teach people about caring!

It takes rare guts and deep caring to be willing to live in the middle of such despair and to make it positive. These are values that are learned in a changing world with changing terms. Maybe the little wart on otherwise healthy Baby Johnny doesn't really matter so much, or the fact that A-OK Baby Susie is a bit more temperamental than you'd like really isn't such a big deal.

It wouldn't be a bad idea for any parent to get in touch with disadvantaged kids today. More and more hospitals in big cities have volunteer programs asking adults to come and hold an AIDS baby or a crack cocaine baby for just an hour per week. Crack babies have the shakes so bad that the only thing that calms them is to have somebody hug them. You could spare one hour, couldn't you? You might want to give it a thought. Moments like that give caring a whole new meaning.

TEAMWORK

Teamwork is the starting point for treating people right. Most people think that teamwork is only important when competing against other teams. I don't. Competition is only part of the teamwork picture. In most things we do in life, people have to work together rather than against each other to get something done. So, I think win-win situations and partnerships are the most important part of teamwork. The best teams in the world are the ones that help people become better and achieve more than they ever thought they could on their own, so it's no mystery that teamwork is such a big part of success.

One place people learn teamwork from is their families. Children get their first teamwork lesson from the way they watch their parents behave toward each other. So, if you're a parent, you are also a teacher of teamwork—good or bad— every day. Your offspring learn from what you do.

For me, the people I've worked with became my family too. Throughout my career, these "second families" have taught me a whole bunch about teamwork.

There are little teams and there are big teams. Your community is a team, for example, just as much as your family is. My daughter Pam organizes volunteer work for the city of Columbus, so she knows a lot about how to get different kinds of teams to work together—from recreation centers to hospital boards. Teams can work together; and teams can compete, too, even when they're not rivals. How come Pam's kids aren't jealous when she spends plenty of time on community work? Simple answer: The kids are all involved in community work themselves and have been from an early age. Pam and her husband Steve endorse it. The community team isn't a rival or an opponent of the family team—it's an extension of it. Neat idea, don't you think?

HEART OF THE HURRICANE

It was 5:00 P.M. Monday morning August 24, 1992, when Hurricane Andrew slammed into South Florida. That day Wendy's got involved in an approach to a community crisis that was very different from anything I had known before. All but three of our twenty-one restaurants in the area were open for business by Friday of that week, and those three were pretty much demolished.

We had employees who lost homes and cars. You know what? Nearly all of them came in to work. *That's terrific,* I thought to myself. *Where else in the world would you find such loyal employees?*

But there's another reason that they came to work, too. Mark Reed, our regional director of operations, pointed out to me that other stuff was at stake for these folks. When your life has turned into chaos, people really like the stability of a job and being part of a team of people whom they can work with. So, if you say to people, "Go home and take care of your own problems," you may actually take away something they need even more.

When a crisis hits, more and more communities realize that quick-service restaurants are some of the best locations to feed disaster victims. After all, we're fast, people know us and our products, and they like the food. Wendy's sent down two "Wendy's on Wheels" units from Columbus. McDonald's and Wendy's each donated about 70,000 to 75,000 free meals during the peak of the crisis. But the best part was that McDonald's and Wendy's worked together. We set up shop next to each other. When Wendy's shut down to regroup, McDonald's began to pick up the slack. When McDonald's shut down, it was vice versa. We even traded employees during a big rush. And our vendors really rallied behind us.

The Wendy's-McDonald's tag team kind of reminds me of *Miracle on 34th Street* when Edmund Gwenn—who plays

Macy's Santa Claus—sends customers over to Macy's rival Gimbel's when Gimbel's has something Macy's has run out of.

Disasters like Hurricane Andrew make it clear that the community sometimes expects more of us, and we better be ready to behave that way. It also doesn't hurt to have disaster reflexes:

- Our primary meat distributor immediately had trucks haul down emergency power generators from Atlanta to help chill food that needed refrigeration. Smart move. We didn't even know they would be needed, but they were.

- We set up special procedures so that people could be paid in cash. In some cases, the restaurant was gone, so people couldn't get their checks. In as many cases, the local bank was blown away so you couldn't cash the check if you had it.

- Our employees filled two eighteen-wheelers with clothes, sleeping bags, and mattresses and shipped them down to Florida.

- We set up a hotline to help fill the needs of Wendy's employees caught in the crisis.

A disaster means that things today aren't the same as things were yesterday. When you read about disasters in the papers, the spotlight is always on the looting and the big bucks insurance companies have to pay out. To me, the stories that we should really pay attention to are the ones about how people help each other out.

We all put a big price tag on being rugged individualists in our country. I know that I do. But this experience really drove home the importance of teamwork to me and to plenty of other people. A hurricane or a tornado may rob you of your home, but it can feel pretty good on the dreary, lonely, break-your-heart morning after a catastrophe to come home to a team to which you belong. Wouldn't you agree? It's "family" written in big letters.

THE REAL DREAM TEAMS

I once asked Lou Holtz, Notre Dame's football coach, universally regarded as one of the top college coaches of our day, "How do you motivate your players, especially when the people you're trying to motivate aren't superstars but more or less average people?"

He said the first thing was to associate yourself with people who care. The team must make the welfare of the organization the top concern. What will get it to do so? "It's the desire to be part of something special," Lou believes. This thought is really important if you want to get to the bottom of success and motivation. Someone may not be a really exceptional performer on his or her own, but everyone wants to share in being a part of something that's special.

The second thing Lou said was that people can be motivated only if the standards are right. They have to have high standards, but they also have to be real ones—standards "that can be achieved with hard work and dedication." People "want to rise above average," he believes, "but if people think that the standards are too high, they won't even try." They'll be frustrated or will lose interest.

The third point he made was, "You cannot motivate anybody who is on drugs or who has a drinking problem. You are just wasting your time."

There are two kinds of dream teams. The first kind gets something done for itself. It succeeds at being the best it can possibly be. Lately, the Dallas Cowboys have been a football dream team, and so was the basketball team that the U.S. sent to the Summer Olympics in 1992. Teamwork is also what it's all about in the Japanese auto industry with companies like Honda, Toyota, and Nissan; and they're teaching the smarts of teamwork to car makers all over the world including our very own auto industry right here in the United States. These are all examples of the first type of dream team. My hat goes off to them.

There's a second type of dream team, too. It aims for something more. It may have an obvious purpose—like being in athletics, or teaching, or research—but it also has a bigger goal. *It's a team that lets its members reach for their dreams and lets them be bigger than any one member could hope to be alone.* They're teams that have a second mission to teach confidence, goodness, and doing the right thing.

I have three dream teams in mind right now. They have one thing in common. They all make music. My idea of a musical dream team is not the Beatles or the Boston Symphony—good as they may have been or may be today. My three picks all happen to be choirs, and they each use music to get to something more, to get to this bigger goal.

If you saw the Steve Martin movie *Leap of Faith* or heard the soundtrack from it, you heard a choir singing a version of Psalm 27. The original version of the song appears on an album by a choir called the Soul Children of Chicago. Walt Whitman heads up Soul Children and has done so since the group was founded twelve years ago.

There are about one hundred African-American boys and girls in the choir—some as young as seven, others as old as seventeen. Some may come from well-to-do areas around Chicago like Barrington, but most join Soul Children from the tough neighborhoods of the South Side and the projects. The kids all have talent, and each auditions to join the choir, so they're gifted to begin with. But Walt and the other people who oversee Soul Children make sure that the choir members live up to other standards, too. Boys who hang out with gangs are out. Kids who do drugs can't be a part of Soul Children. Neither can girls who become pregnant. If school grades slip badly, it's no dice for that singer staying with the group.

This group is good by any standards. Their songs are so

uplifting and inspiring I feel great whenever I hear them. We've invited them to kick off business meetings with their songs. They have three recordings and a video out and they've toured America and Holland, and were a big hit on the White House Christmas Special. In the summer of 1994, they sang the theme song at the World Soccer Championship in Chicago—before two billion people worldwide.

I asked Walt Whitman about the special magic that comes out of Soul Children. Often, it isn't on the stage or even in the music that Soul Children sing. Within Soul Children, the group has its leaders and strong personalities, as every group does. Walt says, though, that he sees kids who are *not* leaders in Soul Children often become leaders back in their schools or in their neighborhoods.

What makes this happen? Soul Children teaches each youngster in the choir—through example and direct, living-flesh contact—how they can be leaders in other things they do in life. It gives them three things, he says, "self-esteem, discipline, and structure."

So what's the main purpose of Soul Children? Is it to sing music? Yes . . . and no. I think that the real goal is bigger. I think that just being in the choir and having to live up to its standards lets every member of that team go after a higher dream.

Harlem in New York City also has a choir, the Boys' Choir of Harlem. It's a lot like Soul Children in many ways, but its music ranges from Bach to Duke Ellington to gospel to hip-hop. The Harlem group was started back in 1968 by a Mississippi music teacher named Dr. Walter Turnbull, who grew up in Mississippi, went to Tougaloo College and then to the Manhattan Institute of Music. He seemed headed for a career as an operatic tenor before another calling grabbed him by the collar.

There are more than 250 young men ages eight to eighteen in the Boys' Choir of Harlem. They, too, have toured all over the U.S. and even gone to Europe and Asia. The kids come from the roughest neighborhoods in New York and seventy-five percent of them are being raised in single female households, but they have to keep a B average to travel and more than ninety-eight percent go on to college. This is in a community where fifty percent of the kids drop out by the tenth grade. Rehearsals are tough, and every rehearsal is followed by group prayers. The Boys' Choir is now the heart of a co-ed Choir Academy of Harlem.[1]

Dr. Turnbull believes, "To be good as a musician, to be good at anything coming from a tough environment, you have to be disciplined." Discipline may be one of the best kinds of support one human being can give another—especially a parent to a child—because good, constructive discipline says "You can do better, and let me show you how." Real support shouts out *"I believe you've got it in you and here's how."*

Walter Turnbull's brother, Horace, who is the organization's business manager today, said that Walter's practice of caring for people started at a very early age. Their mother, Lena, was a single parent and had to work two jobs, so she relied on Walter to guide the children as they were growing up. Walter kept on top of things. He made sure that the chores got done and that everybody's homework was finished in a responsible way.

Walter carried this kind of caring over to the academy and the choir of today. Dr. Turnbull is so keen on manners and values he'll even stop a rehearsal cold if he sees that the kids are starting to walk, talk, or move in an arrogant way—or in any way that is out of sorts with the choir's goal—and they start a rap session about what it means to be a team and the support that they have to give each other to make that team work right.

---

1. "On Wings of Song," The Economist, Dec. 25, 1993.

What's the real purpose of the Boys' Choir of Harlem? Again, I think that music and entertainment are the short side of the story. The real deal here is discipline, self-esteem, and lifting people up. I kind of see Boys' Choir of Harlem as a next step—and an even bigger step—out of the ghetto for its members than another Harlem team that came on the scene years ago: The Harlem Globetrotters. Both are exceptional teams and have been terrific ambassadors.

Well done, Dr. Walter Turnbull!

My third team—and maybe my favorite one of all—is called the Miracles. Their home is the Baddour Memorial Center in Senatobia, Mississippi—about thirty miles from Memphis, Tennessee. The Miracles have around twenty members and their director and guardian angel is a lady named Suzanne Noble. The choir members sing church music and other kinds of songs, too, and they sing their numbers in four-part harmony.

So, what's so special? The Miracles are all mentally challenged adults. If you talked with some of them one on one, they might have a hard time carrying on a conversation with you. Together, however, they are outstanding. They are the pride of Baddour, which is home to about 160 mentally challenged adults. Some of them are as young as eighteen, and others are as old as sixty-eight. Forty-five Sundays a year, the Miracles are on the road performing. When the late Dr. Norman Vincent Peale brought the group to Marble Collegiate Church in New York, he was really moved and said, "We were all thrilled. . . . Not only was the music outstanding, but the members of the choir themselves were so fine."

The thing I like best about the Miracles is that singing in the choir is moonlighting. They all hold down regular jobs in the Center—all the residents of Baddour do. And it's real work.

They assemble new client starter kits for Federal Express, package items for Johnstone and Chromcraft, and operate a horticulture program that is unbelievable. They make their own beds in the morning, and chapel at 7:00 A.M. is a must. They get weekly paychecks. They live in basically normal home units. And residents who put in the effort and the discipline can "graduate" to less and less supervised living. Some live in home settings with no supervision at all.

When the Miracles are on stage they're so proud! The choir appears in bright blazers with slacks or skirts. They even have tuxes for the gents and beaded sweaters and long skirts for the ladies for special occasions. Your heart gets tugged real hard when they end their concert with the song "My Tribute"—as they always do.

I asked a long-time Center employee, what makes the Miracles touch audiences so deeply. In her rich southern drawl, she put her finger on it in a flash: "They love from the h-e-a-r-t. Audiences immediately sense the pure love that accepts everyone just as they are."

We should learn from the Miracles' clear focus. They've put together the work ethic, discipline, and convictions to do what they do. Any of these groups could add some big-time soloist, but what really carries them—for themselves and for others—is what they do as a tight-knit unit.

Sure, I could have made these points about successful teams and talked about the slickest pro baseball team or the Green Berets. But many of these teams—as fine as they are— don't have the fundamentals down as well as these three choirs do, and most of these choir members have fought the over- whelming odds. They learned that "we" is always bigger than "me," no ifs, ands, or buts, and they let this attitude spill over into everything they do.

The values these teams have may be simple, and they may be understood more in the heart than in the head, but they are what make teamwork possible.

Whenever you have people with no natural reason to get

along, let alone to boost themselves up, think of what making them into a team could do. Find somebody to lead them who can turn them into something special. Father Flanagan did it for Boys Town. Willie Nelson pulled a bunch of great musicians together to help the farmers out with Farm Aid. Jimmy Carter and Millard Fuller have done it with Habitat for Humanity by building housing for the poor. I've heard about a racially integrated bowling team that has done more to straighten out race relations in one West Coast town than a whole platoon of psychologists and social workers. What team can you help create that will lift up your office or your neighborhood, your school or your church? What extra-special goal will that team achieve? What dream can it serve?

P.S.: I have to 'fess up, too—there is one other reason that these choirs are among my very favorite teams: envy. I can't sing a lick of music.

THE HERO IS SOMEBODY ELSE

"Roll video. Roll cameras. Background action. Dolly in! Action!

"Oh no, Dave, not again! Cut!" Billy Calhoun—known to most of you as Cousin Ed from the Wendy's commercials has just skated onto the set in a blue ballerina's tutu and hollered out, "Hey, Cuz—you still lookin' for a partner?" Seeing Cousin Ed in this goofy outfit cracked me up so badly that they had to stop filming because I just couldn't stop laughing.

We were shooting commercials in November 1993 for ads that would be aired in February 1994, during the Winter Olympics in Lillehammer, Norway. If you saw the commercial, you know that I had just turned down Kristi Yamaguchi for my pairs figure skating partner as I compete for the gold. (She's a really nice person and a fabulous skater, and she looked kind of down after my decision, so I cooked her up a double hamburger with cheese before she left the set.)

The hero of Wendy's advertising is the product itself. Charlie Rath—our head of advertising who has been such a big factor in mapping out our ad strategy along with Don Calhoon—will tell you that in a flash. Hero? Not me. Not now and never will be. You gotta start off with the question of talent. The truth is I don't have any talent as an actor. Zero.

I remember the creative director Paul Basile, a super pro from our agency, Bates Worldwide, telling me when we first started shooting ads, "Just try being yourself." Then, fifty-six takes later, our director, Billy Hudson, came up to me. He always wears this red baseball cap and he was tugging on it so hard I thought his head would pop through it. "Dave," he pleaded, "why don't you try being somebody else?" I've done about three hundred commercials so far, and a lady last week walked up to me and asked, "Dave, do you think that you'll ever get one right?"

Billy Hudson is a genius, especially at lighting. He's also good at keeping the attitudes up for people on the set. He supports them. They support him. Commercials are expensive to make, and you need a lot of people. One of our marketing people said that it's like watching very expensive paint dry. Billy only works with the best—like producer Sabrina Palladino and assistant director Loren Frank.

Jim McKennan writes the lines, and is he ever great. He makes the lines try to fit me, rather than trying to shoehorn me into the ad copy—and I can't tell you how important that is. Helga Petrashevich has the job of making sure that the script is organized for all the changes on the set. John Hirst is the sound guy who makes sure that everything that is said gets recorded. John has a way of making you appreciate the importance of sound. "Ahhhh," he'll say, "without the sound, all you have is the Mona Lisa." I always kid Sal Guida, our cameraman, to make sure I won't have a double chin in the shot.

We even have a little troupe of actors, who you'll recognize from commercial to commercial. Joe Sirola is the invisible announcer's voice who is in every commercial. Skip

Chertoff is one of the extras. He's the guy who catches me after I catch the medicine ball in one of the ads where I wear a sweatshirt and say, "You know what I like about exercise? When it's *over!*"

One of our extras even got asked for an autograph by a youngster at a Wendy's restaurant because the extra was in a Wendy's ad. (He had traveled with the Radio City Rockettes for one year, and nobody asked him for an autograph back then.) He rose to the occasion like a real professional, I might add. "Bring me your hamburger, young man," he said, "and I shall sign it in ketchup."

Donna Moyer handles my hair and makeup. We don't use much makeup because Billy thinks that the lighting should carry how people look, and I agree. Donna is responsible for seeing that my cheeks are rosy from one take to the next and for getting the oil out of my hair. Vegetable oil, no lie! I thought that I left that problem behind me when I stopped being a grill man.

Bob Levite—who is with our agency and is a pretty good photographer in his own right—says that a mixture of vegetable oil and carbon dioxide, which a cooker with a fan turns into smoke, is harmless and gives the lighting on the set a warm glow. I appreciate that, but Dolores Zaccaro and Miriam Tsao—who handle my wardrobe as well as Michael Douglas's and Kevin Costner's—always complain about how much oil gets soaked up in the clothes. Believe ol' Dave, an advertising shoot can surely mess up one fine set of polyester threads.

The most important person who handles the appearance of things is Midori Matsumoto. She's responsible for seeing that the Wendy's food in the commercials looks just like it does in the restaurants. Forget about me—the real hero always gets the girl (er, grill).

As a team, these people all have tremendous respect for each other. An electrician will get you a glass of water, and a boom operator might help you straighten up your tie. With the union rules in the entertainment industry, that kind of flexibility is very rare. When an ending isn't right, the team stops everything to fix it. Then we film until we get it right.

These folks are my pals—guys like the grip man (that's a stagehand, you know) Jim Turner; Dan Mahon, who handles props; and Matt Dee, Wendy's producer who works for Charlie and Don as kind of a general coordinator. We treat each other like family. We have fun at what we're doing. And we believe in quality all the way around—except for the acting ability of yours truly, of course.

All the people who help make our advertising successful on the set, in the cutting rooms, or in the traffic department that schedules the ads—they're great folks. There is also a team behind the scenes, involved in planning for new product development, training, and lots of other things. But do you know who I think are the real heroes of our advertising? The franchisees. The local operators. The people behind the grills and counters of the restaurants. After all, an ad may make your mouth water, but you can't eat it.

<u>Support</u>

Many people believe that support is something you give someone you feel sorry for or that it means propping somebody up who would fail unless you were there to give him a boost. No sir, that's not how I see it. That's caring, and caring is different than support. Caring is what you give people who need help. Support is the boost you give people who can help themselves but who need a partner to open a window or to push aside a roadblock. Support isn't a bunch of reckless advice, either. It's real help—commitment and effort. Support is "teamwork plus." Support is also sharing feelings and insights with other people. It's helping others with their awareness and making your own awareness stronger at the same time.

The best way to get support is to give it. Wendy's president Gordon Teter likes to remind people of a saying that Jack Mollenkopf, his college coach at Purdue, often used: "Meet me halfway, and it's amazing what can happen." It is amazing what can be done when you treat people with respect. Respect goes both ways, too. Just as the players need it from the coach, the coach needs it from the players.

Support is also easier if things aren't too complicated. Gordon believes in what he calls "The Law of the Lowest Common Denominator," and it has nothing to do with 'rithmetic. It goes like this: "The simpler you can keep it, the better you can execute it." It's that way for a department and their boss, for a congregation and their minister, for a bunch of volunteers and their chairperson. If you want to give and get support, it's a lot more likely to come and keep coming if the rules are simple and clear than if they're fuzzy and complicated.

THE FAMILY THAT TALKS TOGETHER

People know that I'm big on families and on values because I'm traditional. They see me in T.V. ads cruising in a Chrysler New Yorker convertible or wearing a flannel shirt or sitting in a living room straight out of the fifties, and they say, "There's old-fashioned Dave." But I've got good news for all you folks who may look at life pretty much like I do: All our fancy market research indicates that people in the '90s are looking to the family more and more as "a place of refuge and revitalization."[1]

Plenty of people born during the Baby Boom that followed World War II are now taking a second look at organized religion. People really want their homes today to be comfortable and usable and not put together to show off a dining-room table or a living-room sofa that are used only a couple times a year. Home is where they want to spend their leisure hours.

When I grew up, like most of the people in my generation, the biggest family event of the day was evening dinner. Since both my adoptive parents worked, we usually didn't eat until late, but at least we ate together. Most of the time, my parents did the talking. It could have been about work or money or politics, and sometimes we kids were bored with it all—but it was communication, and it was pretty regular. After dinner, we might listen to Bob Hope or Jack Benny on the radio or hear Walter Winchell tapping on his telegraph as he sent his messages out to Mr. and Mrs. America, and then it was bedtime.

Time together like that doesn't happen as often today. Kids play basketball or soccer at school or they help out at the community center or they may have some kind of part-time work. (Our studies tell us that fewer than half of all families eat together seven nights a week.) They don't eat together much; they talk with each other even less. More than forty percent of the time spent eating at home is done while watching the VCR

---

1. Bates Worldwide research, 1993.

or the T.V. We know more about Michael Jackson and Michael Jordan than we know about our own families. That's not very encouraging.

I did a little of my own research last week and talked with some of my younger friends who are raising teenagers. Too often children and parents talk to each other today through notes left on those little yellow stickers people slap on the door of their refrigerators or through the messages that get left on the answering machine. You might not like that. I know I don't. Face-to-face is best, but you can also do a better job of using answering machines when you just can't be there in person.

Here's just one example. I was in an airport last week and overheard a woman leaving a message for a youngster. I didn't mean to eavesdrop, but she was doing such a good job of leaving a message that I couldn't help myself. She said that she was sorry that she wouldn't be there to take him to Little League practice when he came home from school but that she had set it up with a neighbor to have him picked up at 3:45. He could find milk and cookies in the refrigerator. She said that she wanted to take a look at his math and science homework that evening. Then she finished up by saying that she loved him and that she was sure he'd do a super job of shagging pop flies at Little League practice. She went through everything in a slow, clear, warm way.

I thought to myself, *Maybe it isn't answering machines and voice mail that are such a problem. If we stopped acting as if we were shouting an order on the floor of the stock exchange, perhaps answering machines wouldn't be so bad after all.*

But answering machines and yellow stickers aren't the perfect answer, and we all know it. Try to carve out one meal a week (once a day is the best) where you all eat together and where you all talk with each other instead of watching *CNN* or *Wheel of Fortune.* That one dinner—and it doesn't have to be at an old-fashioned hamburger restaurant, although I can recommend a good one—may actually be more important than basketball practice or ceramics class.

We talk about child and family neglect all the time. Some of that neglect is gross and ugly. Some of it is a lot less obvious. It comes from the best intentions of trying to do too much—but it can kill a family just like creeping crabgrass can kill a lawn.

SOME ADVICE ON SUCCESSFUL ADVICE

To Kenny King, Sr., sobriety was success. It was his number-one, unequaled success in life. I met Kenny King about thirty years ago when he owned more than twenty restaurants in Cleveland. Kenny was a wealthy man and achieved a great deal in his life by anybody's standards. But of all the things that Kenny could be proud of, the one thing that he was the proudest of all about was staying sober. For thirty years he was off booze, and he made that leap, he often told me, one step before he would have sunk into the gutter and ruined his life and his family's, too. Kenny chose not to be anonymous about his own alcoholism in order to set a leadership example. Even after thirty years, he would still devotedly go to Alcoholics Anonymous meetings every week and sometimes more often. Here was a guy who very nearly had a broken life helping *me* out—someone who came from a broken home life—and it all worked out okay. Maybe what the Bible has to say about the value of "broken vessels" really is true.

After a while I started to go with him to AA meetings. Not because I had a drinking problem—I don't even like to drink very much—but because Kenny invited me. Alcoholics Anonymous is one of the best and certainly has been one of the most effective examples of people helping people. Alcoholism is serious trouble in our country. Eighteen million Americans are problem drinkers. Of these, 10.5 million are bona fide alcoholics.

People ask me if I go to church regularly. It's a little embarrassing to admit it, but the honest answer is no—at least not in the strictest sense of the word.

But, yes I do, if you look at it another way. In my opinion, the church that works for me has no building, no choir, no pulpit, no communion, no altar, no formal congregation. For years now I have tried to find "church" in being around people who support each other and hold each other accountable. This has surely been true at Wendy's and a lot of other organizations I have been involved in. But, I really learned the importance of this through showing up as a guest at AA years ago. It's been decades since I've been to an AA meeting, but the impression made on me by the few I attended was really deep.

The right way to look at AA, I think, is as a church where the congregation is anonymous. Church—as I understand the old-time definition—is getting together for a good reason. AA is not designed for sight-seeing or listing people in *Who's Who*. It's joining with other people to do a little self check-up, some reflection, and a tad of confidence building. At AA everybody is welcome. Most important of all, everyone is equal. It's one of the finest combinations of group-help and self-help that I know of.

There is good news in the alcohol story. Programs like Alcoholics Anonymous are working. I'm told that in just the past quarter century, the amount people drink is down a remarkable twenty percent. We learned from the experiences of the 1920s that prohibition is not the way to tackle problem drinking in our society. Education and self-control are the way to do it.

I have read through the twelve simple steps of the Alcoholics Anonymous program many times. Two stick out in my mind, steps five and six: "We admitted to God, to ourselves and to another human being the exact nature of our wrongs," and "We were entirely ready to have God remove all these defects of character."

These two steps are really worth keeping in mind if you

are trying to overcome what people call character flaws. First, if you don't level—I mean really level—with God, with yourself, and with at least one other human being, you will never succeed in overcoming the problem. Otherwise, when the next temptation comes along, you can always deny that the problem really exists.

Second, you have to be ready to let God into the act to straighten things up. If you have a problem now, what makes you think that you can fix it all by your lonesome? I strongly believe that success would be so much more within our reach if we shared more about our flaws with others and asked for their help in straightening us out.

Some people think that AA is where folks go to share advice. I don't. I think that it's where people go to share *awareness*. There is a big difference between awareness and advice. You have to be careful about where you go for advice and how seriously you take it. Watch out for people who offer advice and who have absolutely nothing to lose if the advice they give doesn't work:

- "Leave the jerk! You've deserved somebody better ever since the baker chilled the frosting on your wedding cake fifteen years ago."

- "Go ahead and take that whirl on South African mining stocks. You know, I was reading in the tabloid by the grocery checkout the other day. . . ."

- "Stand up for your rights and tell your boss a thing or two. By gosh, they're lucky to have you in that department. . . ."

That kind of advice may make you feel good when you get it, but the truth could be that hubby ain't that much of a jerk, that the quality of investment advice in that rag isn't worth wrapping fish in, and that there are three people lined up to take your job if you go ahead and tell off the boss.

Kenny King really mastered the art of support. I'm convinced that because of what he learned at AA, he knew how to listen without letting his own views get tangled in the conversation. That's the way he listened to me when we talked about my business plans for the future. In fact, Kenny King never thought much of quick-service restaurants. He thought that coffee shops were here to say. But he was the most supportive person I knew when I thought through the idea of Wendy's. He just kept encouraging me to use my own common sense, and he had confidence that what I did, I would do successfully. Trust people's advice, but trust common sense and your own confidence, too.

We've made strides in making sure that people are treated fairly in the workplace. Harassment and prejudice happen a lot less often, and that's great. But sometimes the laws have gotten so sticky that it's hard to tell a person where he or she really stands; some bosses spend more time finding words that are not objectionable to "share" with an employee, than finding the right words to help the employee understand how to improve. I'm all for showing respect for employees, but bending over that far backwards kinda garbles what you're trying to say!

The one piece of advice that my family kept trying to give me when Lorraine and I were raising them: "Daddy, please spend more time with us kids." "Daddy, Mr. McGillicuddy is home by five every night, and he's always out there shooting baskets with his kids in the back yard." "Daddy, the Oswalds and the Daytons are going camping out by Cedar Point in Sandusky. Why don't we ever do anything like that?"

I felt guilty that I couldn't spend more time with my children while they were growing up. I felt guilty, but I also felt I was doing the right thing as I look back today on what I did then. In the end, I felt it was more important that I earn the money to feed, clothe, house, and educate my kids right than to pretend I was Ozzie Nelson, from the set of *Ozzie and Harriet*. I bet that a lot of you people feel guilty, too. Most hard-working, God-fearing people are afraid that they cheat their families—the very people they're working hardest to serve—by not paying them enough attention. And today it's a lot harder than it was in the Ozzie and Harriet world since we have so many families where *both* parents must work and are trying to be the best parents *and* the best workers. Personally, I don't know if our family would have had half a chance when we moved to Columbus in the '60s if Lorraine hadn't been there to fill so many roles that I would have liked to been able to fill myself.

That guilt about not being fair to the family—be it dad or mom—may be some of the most unfair guilt people try to shoulder. What manager can say no to the next management meeting or to a crash work session on a weekend? Parents let their kids down and sometimes feel bad about work because of what they've had to do. If I could write permission slips to responsible parents not to feel guilty about "short-changing" their families, I'd write them by the boxcar load. Many fine people have been robbed of their self-confidence as parents and have no real reason to feel that way.

You know how I dealt with guilt about not spending more time with my family? How I handled it in my own head whenever I felt really bad about not doing more for my kids and their pleas? Times like when the Olsen family would come in to pick up some Kentucky Fried Chicken for a picnic while there was Dave splattering himself with grease as he stood over the deep fryer because some short-order cook called in sick on a Saturday afternoon? I would play out a little mental fantasy, a tour I called the "Slum Grand Slam."

I would daydream for a minute that we piled all the kids into the station wagon and drove down to the very worst shacks in all of Columbus. Then I would imagine that I was talking to the kids as we toured this seedy neighborhood, saying, "You know I could be home at five in the evening, and we could play gin rummy till the cows come home, but then you might have to trade those nice wallpapered bedrooms and the pretty curtains of ours for a tar-papered shed and greasy old oilcloth window shades. I could close the restaurants on Saturday, but then I'd probably be out of business. What the heck, I mean you wouldn't mind sharing that single dirty toilet under the landing with the two families across the hall or chowing down a steady diet of canned beans at night or dropping out of school at fifteen or sixteen to get a full-time job to help support the family."

I have to stress that we never took the "Slum Grand Slam" tour, though I thought about it more than once as the family was growing up. Some people might criticize me for even considering it. Right or wrong, it helped me stay focused on what I had to do. Sometimes you have to feel right about sticking with an unpopular decision you have to make, especially if you're the leader and others are depending on you. And, in the end, I think I did mostly the right thing.

Could I have attended a few more school plays, spent a couple more days at the beach, or gone with the kids for a drive or two more and just chatted? Sure, I could have. But success is a funny thing. You make a commitment, and you do it. Balance is important, and you should always strive for it. Balance is what can save both alcoholics and workaholics. But in the world of earning a living, at least, you can never forget to factor in one very powerful truth: *There are very few half-successful people.* The marketplace today is so tough that it just doesn't allow you to be half good.

Homemaker, deacon, shipping foreman, volunteer nurse, shortstop, or librarian, be the best that you can be; and then go the extra mile and put balance in your life. It's *not* easy, and I've probably spent most of my life not being able to balance the needs of work and family. It's not easy, but it's one heck of a goal.

SUPPORT ON THE GO

The average person needs support the most when relocating to a new town—at least that's my experience. In 1962 Lorraine and I moved from Fort Wayne, Indiana, with less than three thousand dollars to our name. Everybody remembers 1962 as the year Khrushchev pulled the Soviet missiles out of Cuba and astronaut John Glenn orbited the earth in the "Friendship 7" space capsule. Khrushchev was knocked out of power just two years later. John Glenn and I were luckier. We both landed in Ohio. He became a U.S. senator and I wound up in the quick-service food industry. I don't know which of us saw the more different landscape: John Glenn coming to Ohio from outer space or me moving to Columbus from Fort Wayne. I only know that this move was the shock of a lifetime for me.

Columbus is a much bigger city than Fort Wayne, and it was so even back then. Today Columbus is the biggest city in all of Ohio. For years, Columbus had been the banking and trading center for a huge farming region that targeted corn, wheat, and soybeans as its cash crops. Columbus was also a rail town. Union Station downtown was a big-city train terminal; at one time, five trunk lines ran through Columbus. One of the city's top manufacturing firms made railroad train cars themselves. Columbus is also the home of Ohio State University— the nation's biggest single-campus state school. Today, Ohio State has more than 52,000 students and is much larger, for example, than either UCLA or the University of Minnesota.

When I arrived in Columbus, the old University Hall was still standing. It has since been torn down and rebuilt. Those beautiful carillon chimes had been ringing for years from the tower of Orton Hall, but the biggest sound in all Columbus was the roar of 90,000 people jammed into Ohio Stadium to watch the Buckeye football team under coach Woody Hayes. Not just for football, OSU had and still has a big influence on the feel of Columbus.

The other strong force that influenced the character of Columbus was (and remains) politics, since it's the state capital. Involvement with our government leaders was a brand new ball game for me. Of course, the business was the biggest thing for me, but I tried to get involved in the community, too.

Before long, I was appointed to a blue-ribbon committee by the mayor. To this day, I'm not sure I can tell you what the committee did. As I explained in *Dave's Way*, I would take free samples of Kentucky Fried Chicken down to local T.V. and radio stations and barter the food for some free air time to talk about our chicken.

I was pretty young and aggressive, but most of all I was afraid. I was afraid that I would go down as just another could-have-been, trying to support a family with then four kids, mopping up coffee spills on a lunch counter or working as a grill man. Although I tried to make myself more visible in the community, I mostly stuck around people I felt comfortable with. The first people I got to know ran small businesses. The earliest Columbus friends I made were my air conditioning vendor, a couple of guys at the corner gas station, and my chicken supplier.

By just looking around me and trying to figure out what was going on, by not being afraid to take a risk and promote the business, and by making a few loyal friendships, I was able to make progress fast. Although Columbus was a big new world for me, I tried to let it change me as little as possible. The support I looked for and got came from basic, ordinary people just like the folks I had known back in Knoxville and Fort Wayne.

Even today, the most important support I get is from people who have great common sense. Wendy's CEO Jim Near is one of the most supportive business partners a person could hope for because he cares and has the best common sense I've ever seen on two feet. The support of good business partners in my early days in Columbus helped take care of me and plant my feet in the community, but what about the rest of my family? When do family members need to support each other?

Well, like I said earlier, relocations are among the hardest experiences any family must face. When we moved to Columbus I was thankful that Lorraine shouldered as much as she did for all of us. A move may be an opportunity, and that's what I felt our move to Columbus would turn out to be. But with both spouses working, it's a lot harder for many families these days.

Back in the '60s I thought moving was simple. You took a little group of people called a family, bundled up their belongings, lifted them out of one city and dropped them into another. As many of you know, that's not the way it usually works. These days moving is a big issue, because people are moving all the time as they change jobs or companies. But years ago, people mostly made moves to get ahead in their careers, and they were the exception not the rule. Today more and more moves are made simply to stay in place—to stick with a certain company or just to get a job when the old company cuts back. So you had better know how to break camp and gallop off.

Many people—maybe most—make moves badly because they don't know how to execute a move. End result: they mess up what has become a survival skill today. In a way, I was lucky when I grew up because my early days were spent as a nomad. Caravan Dave they called me. I went to three or four different schools in a single year. It didn't help my education much—that's for sure—but it sure as heck made me adaptable.

The first piece of advice I have about moving is the hardest to follow, and that's to travel light in life. If you are the kind of person who falls in love with things—bookcases, chests of drawers, patio furniture, snowshoes—you will soon find out that the rock gardens and china cabinets of life don't love back, especially if you have to take them somewhere.

Do you think that I own more stuff than I need to or should today? I choke on my junk—like most of America. But I'm proud of one bloodless streak in me: I'm more ruthless than Deadeye Dick in cutting loose things I own. Every day, you have to snap that bullwhip in your head and threaten the things around you. "Now hear this, rocking chair and all you other heirlooms: I own you. You don't own me."

My second piece of advice is to not go into a move thinking that it's going to be a picnic. When people relocate for the first time, their eyes get big as they hear about "The Package." The package, they think, is some box of goodies that Santa just dumped off on their back porch. The package is what business people call the special money and benefit parts of the move: house-hunting trip, moving expenses, and all the other incidentals. Good employers offer good packages, and a smart person will ask for a fair one. But you have to realize that no package is going to buy you a smooth relocation if you don't get involved in making it work.

In simpler (I'm not saying fairer) times, when moves were fewer, the stock solution was to let the wife worry about the relocation. Lorraine had the real responsibility for making our relocation to Columbus work. She moved into a house that she had never even seen. But she'll tell you that at least we were lucky that our kids weren't teenagers—it's a lot easier to move younger kids than it is teenagers, with all the friendships they make and the activities they have.

With so many dual wage earners in families today, the spouse who is the cause for the relocation is as likely to be a woman as a man. A hidden problem can creep up if the "caboose" spouse (personnel pros actually call this person the "trailing spouse") in the move feels short-changed. It's called the "you owe me one" disease. It's a disease that can fester for years, and one day it'll pop out of its shell like a baby dragon: "You owe me a better house," "I get the next career move," and the last song is often "I'm gonna get me a lawyer."

Another mistake people make is what I call "The Clean Start Dream." People often start snoozing into this dream before or just after they go through a divorce. Clean-start snoring sounds like this: "Since we're breaking up and the kids will live with their mother in Milwaukee, I've always wanted to give it a go in a town like Santa Fe. . . ." The rest of that story ends with ". . . and they lived happily ever after." But that's only a story. The real world is often quite different.

A third problem in relocation is assuming that the same standards apply everywhere. Schools are a great example of this. I know a family who had their kids in the best public school in the suburbs of a big city, and their youngsters were at the head of the class in everything. They moved to Minneapolis and insisted on finding a home near the very best public school in the suburban Twin Cities. School's great, but the kids aren't doing well. They're struggling to keep up with the new academic standards, as they're much higher than the old ones were.

Regina Robbins is a professional who specializes in executive relocations. The firm she is with is one of the best in the business. It's called Relocation Resources, and it's based in Boston. Regina has the same opinion as my wife Lorraine: families with teenagers generally have the toughest relocation problems.

Regina also mentions two things that best predict if a move will be a success: First, is this a healthy family with a good marriage? If the relocation counselor starts to learn a bunch of things from the husband and wife separately other than what the couple shares with the counselor when they're together, that's a warning sign that communication is bad, and the marriage is probably not much better.

Second, if the relocated person doesn't respect the company they are or will be working for, that's another likely tip-off of trouble on the horizon.

Am I against relocations? No way. That's the way business runs today and for the future, as far as I can see it. But you have to keep things in focus. What will this move do to my spouse? What will it do to our children and their education? Relocations rarely solve problems and may create a few.

So use your head, talk it out, keep a leash on your possessions, and support family members as they weather this difficult transition. If you do that, the long-term value of a smart relocation could well be worth it. In my case, I'm sure glad we moved. It turned out to be the cherry on the whipped cream as far as I was concerned.

PART THREE

UPWARD: GOING FOR EXCELLENCE AND BEYOND

When you have your own act together and get along well with others, you're ready to reach for another plateau, that of excellence.

Nothing is as tricky in the world of success as excellence. From our earliest days, we are taught that it is snazzy, glossy, bigger than life. It's that three seconds of glory when a major leaguer puts one out of the park or a figure skater completes a triple axel, not the constant training or workouts. But that's just false. Most people think excellence in business is sitting at a big desk and making power decisions, but true excellence is really the years beforehand making little and big right decisions and learning from mistakes when things go wrong.

No one can excel in everything. In fact, excellence in any one little thing is hard enough. And don't forget: it's easy to become selfish when you go for the gold. The graveyards of the world are loaded with people who lost it all at the same time they thought they were winning it all.

Motivation

Without a doubt, motivation is a key to success. Know what motivates you and prove to yourself that this motivation is honest and worthwhile. But don't let too many different things motivate you, or you'll be tangled up in a maze of all kinds of conflicts. Stay focused. Figure out what your motivations are going to be in the next step of your life before you arrive at the next step. Keep dreaming, but don't daydream: If you do it for praise, you are likely to short-change yourself in the end. Look at success firsthand so that you really know how it works and what it costs to achieve.

I'm big on lapel pins. Some people hand out business cards; I give away lapel pins. We give out Wendy's pins to employees, and to customers, too—they're just as much a part of the family as anyone else. As I said, I don't believe in wearing your beliefs on your sleeve; I believe in wearing them on your lapel. Yep, I'm one of those guys who'll wear an American flag pin on my lapel from time to time; it shows I'm proud to be an American. In the same way, by wearing Wendy's lapel pins, our employees show they're proud to be part of the Wendy's team. When I meet people for the first time and give them a Wendy's pin, I always ask for their names. I don't do it for effect; I find that asking that question really helps me focus on who I'm talking with. Does having a little symbol that means they're part of the Wendy's family motivate an employee to work a little harder, or a customer to come in more often? A little bit, I'll bet. And success in life is made up of a lot of little bits where you keep yourself motivated and motivate others too.

KEEP THE PROFITS—I WANT TO BE RICH

Before Wendy's was founded, my first true business success was turning around a group of four failing Kentucky Fried Chicken franchises in Columbus, Ohio. How did I do it? There were lots of reasons, I guess, but one sticks with me to this day: It was giving up the profits on the soft-drink machine that may have made me rich.

Especially in summertime, people would come in for Kentucky Fried Chicken as a carry-out item to take along on picnics. I can still remember little Marti from down the block, who would always stand in line with her inflatable seahorse beach toy. When the twin sisters Eunice and Velda, who were about twelve or thirteen, would come in on weekends with their mother, my knuckles would turn white as I gripped the counter by the cash register. Eunice and Velda were knitters, and they were scrappers, too. I was always afraid they'd have a sword fight with their knitting needles right in front of the mashed potatoes.

Cold soda pop, I learned, was the best medicine to keep a lid on tempers and impatience. Folks standing in line waiting for their orders wanted something cold to drink, or they wanted some cold soda pop to take with them. At that time these stores didn't have beverage service behind the counter.

When the soft-drink machine ran out, I could see that customers waiting in line often got impatient and left. It took me weeks to figure out what the real problem was and how to solve it. I was managing the group of restaurants, and *I* wasn't able to take care of the problem—certainly not in four restaurants. But what could I do to motivate the people who *could* do the right thing?

I told the managers of the individual restaurants, "Let's make a deal. You make sure that the vending machine is always full of soft drinks every minute we're open, and you can keep all the profits I'm entitled to from the machine." It worked. The managers were motivated to do the right thing. I wasn't in business to make money off the vending machine; I was in business to make money off chicken. But a lot of people don't see their situation that way; they try to squeeze out the tiniest penny from a side business and forget their main business.

If you take the time to understand your motivation and the motivation of people around you, and then do something sensible to make those motivations work better, life can be ten times easier.

I had a friend during my early restaurant days named Hep, who ran a little dairy store. He used to see me bolting around these restaurants, and you would think that *I* was a chicken running around with its head cut off. I'd be scrubbing pots or dishing up orders, and people on the payroll would be taking a break off in the corner.

"Run your business, son, don't let your business run you!" Hep would say.

I finally figured out what he meant. I had a job—running things—and I wasn't doing it. From that day forward, I told everyone on the team: "Look, I'm always here to help when we get into a jam. But from now on, I'm the last one to ever put on an apron and the first one to take it off." It was really then that I got both my motivations and my priorities straight.

The same principle holds true for successful living as holds true for a successful business. If you do everything in your life equally well, more power to you. In case you haven't figured it out yet, you're one of the very few people in the world who can (and I'm sure not among your number). It all boils down to *motivation with a focus*. When you're working with people, focus means giving people you rely on trust and real responsibility. As long as I worried about soda pop, I couldn't run my restaurants. For parents, as long as they don't give the teenager who is babysitting their kids real trust, how can they ever enjoy a night out? If you don't let junior people in your department try, and maybe fail, on a big assignment, will they ever learn to do a job that's stretching or tough? Give people a chance with the right motivations, and they will make you proud—and may even help make you rich.

THE COLLEGE OF PRACTICAL KNOWLEDGE

People's disposable income—the money they really have jingling in their pocketbooks to spend—climbed in a steady upward march through 1990; then it started to fall off again. That's bad news, especially for the Baby Boomer generation. Baby Boomers feel more pressure than others. One reason why is that they are about to face up to the reality of sending their kids to college. Paying for college is one of the biggest nightmares a middle-aged couple has to deal with these days.

In a "knowledge economy," going to college has become even more important. Even though I've never been to college, I'm on the board of trustees at Duke University. You know what I think is one of the biggest problems today about college? It's not getting *to* college or *through* college, but doing the *planning* to afford to go to college. And I'm not talking about putting aside a war chest the size of the Denver Mint in the hopes that your kids will one day go to Duke or Stanford. To me, it's mostly a question of being motivated to do the right thing.

By the time a youngster turns twelve or thirteen, you should have a pretty good idea if he or she has the interest and the ability to go to college. That's the time the young person's parent or guardian should be sitting down to figure what's doable, affordable, and practical.

Columbus, Ohio has a community program that truly works. It's been working for years, and I personally think it should be copied in every city in America. It's called I Know I Can. This program guarantees that every qualified Columbus high-school graduate who wants to go to college will have the chance at one of seven local colleges or universities, or any other place in the country he or she chooses.

The high-speed locomotive behind I Know I Can is a lady

by the name of Teckie Shackelford. Teckie is one of the most respected community leaders in all of Ohio, and her leadership, enthusiasm, and common sense come through in everything she does. I'm proud to say that Teckie is on Wendy's board of directors. My daughter Pam sees her as a mentor and role model, and many other young men and women in Columbus feel the same way. President Bush cited her as the number-one volunteer in America when he gave her the Ronald Reagan Award and Medal.

No matter what the youngster's financial means may be, I Know I Can stands behind its guarantees. What it offers is "last-dollar financing"—fancy words for covering the difference between what the student can ante up and what the cost of college is.

There's a hitch to this program. And there's beauty to the hitch, too. Students have to exhaust every other source of funding before this last-dollar funding kicks in. They have to be motivated to try to find the money sources, and they have to realize that getting the cash to pay for college is a job just like any other job. Advisors work with the students to make sure that financial-aid forms are filled out properly, and that they are thinking about the right kind of colleges for their interests. Speakers from the community go into the schools and talk to kids at the middle-school level to get them to start thinking early about the possibility of entering the program. More than eight thousand kids have been helped. And, as part of the deal, kids have to give back something themselves by doing some volunteer work for I Know I Can.

One of the program's many success stories is Jeanne Yungfleisch. Jeanne wanted to go to college to become a teacher—a dream she had since she was little. She would be the first person in her family ever to go to college, but she would need scholarship aid. I Know I Can volunteers helped realize Jeanne's dream. She won a scholarship from Ohio Dominican and now teaches at Binns' Elementary in Columbus.

When Larry King asked me on his TV show if Wendy's was third in size compared to the other quick-service chains, I said that we were first in quality, and I truly, truly believe that.

I joined the army when I was 18 and sailed for Germany in 1951.

As a toddler by Gull Lake in Michigan, I got to spend my summers with my adoptive Grandma Minnie. Years later, she had me baptized here.

I learned a whole bunch about the restaurant business in Ft. Wayne, Indiana. My boss, Phil Clauss, was a mentor and a great role model.

The Colonel had a knack for promotion. I used to get him to do radio and newspaper interviews, and appear on TV, all the time thinking, "I'll do anything but stand before a camera." Look at me today.

When Dr. Peale presented the Horatio Alger Award to me in 1979, I was truly humbled to be in the presence of such a great man.

Marrying Lorraine Buskerk was truly one of my smartest moves. Forty years later, we're still a great team.

Lorraine worked hard to make sure that this family photo got taken. Each of the children's families is wearing a different color shirt: Pam's is in lavender, Kenny's is in pink, Molly's is in rose, Wendy's is in dark blue, and Lori's is in light blue.

After I received my GED degree in 1993, Lorraine and I were invited to the Coconut Creek High School prom in Ft. Lauderdale.

We were named honorary King and Queen of the Prom, and I was voted "Most Likely to Succeed."

Here's Lorraine arranging my graduation cap and gown. My GED diploma is proudly displayed in the hallway of our Florida home.

While on my first book tour, we arranged to speak to high school newspaper editors across the country. We wanted to emphasize the importance of staying in school.

I'm really proud that I finished high school, forty-five years after I dropped out.

People sometimes call me the hero of Wendy's advertising. No way. The real heroes are the employees in the restaurants doing a great job every day, like these in Winter Park, Florida.

It's hard for me to go to a Wendy's and not be noticed. Ever since I started being on TV, people have come up to me to talk about our food or commercials.

Ron Fay, a Wendy's franchisee, is an outstanding restaurant operator, and really smart about questions of quality.

Thanks for coming by!

TAKE SIDES

When I visit a Wendy's, I generally try to autograph one of the posters in the restaurant. Employees kind of like having a personal reminder of the founder, I guess.

Eating lunch with Kristi Yamaguchi—Olympic gold medalist and a terrific person. This is on the set for the commercial shoot. For this special occasion, I cooked the hamburgers myself.

Sal Guida takes a light reading at the commercial shoot for our Spicy Chicken Sandwich. We have a wonderful team on the set—like an extended family.

This is part of the team that makes our TV commercials. We've made more than 300 commercials together, and the product is always the hero. From left: Don Calhoon, Bob Levite, Jim McKennan, Billy Hudson, Mike LaGattuta, Paul Basile, Charlie Rath, and Matt Dee.

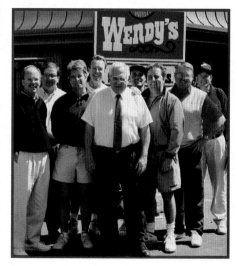

As a kid, I was a big fan of Gene Autry and Roy Rogers, so I was happy to put on western duds for one of our ads.

Wendy's franchisee, Mike Toukan, is just over my right shoulder. Mike can't even ride a motorcycle, but he's right in the ad because he was a leading bidder in a charity auction for adoption.

Jim Near (L) and Gordon Teter are the best operators in the restaurant industry. I love the way we support each other.

The famous actor, Lee Majors, stopped by one of our commercial shoots in Miami. He's a great guy—six million dollars worth!

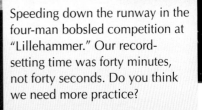

Speeding down the runway in the four-man bobsled competition at "Lillehammer." Our record-setting time was forty minutes, not forty seconds. Do you think we need more practice?

"The Miracles" choir from Senatobia, Mississippi. The late Dr. Norman Vincent Peale praised both the quality of these people as well as the excellence of their music.

The kids at St. Jude's Ranch in Nevada do a terrific job recycling greeting cards. It's great training in work ethic and a good fundraiser for the Ranch.

Wendy's franchisee, Joe Karam (L) and two driving forces behind St. Jude's Ranch–Nola Helm and Father Herbert Ward.

The Soul Children of Chicago are an outstanding musical group, led by Walt Whitman. Being part of this choir teaches discipline and teamwork, too.

Here I am with Mattie Hart and three of her kids. Mattie drives a school bus and has a heart of solid gold.

In total, Mattie and her husband have adopted eleven children in addition to raising five birth children.

Orlando Magic General Manager, Pat Williams and his wife, Jill, have eighteen children—four birth children and fourteen adopted ones, but Pat says he can't remember which are which.

This is the dinner table in the Williams' home—the longest one I've ever seen. It was a real honor to be in a home that combines such love and discipline.

Think you have a challenge raising your family? I know I thought I did, but imagine a household with seven thirteen-year-olds!

The Child Welfare League of America gave me their top award. Dionne Warwick and Miss America, Kimberly Aiken, joined in the festivities.

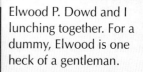

Elwood P. Dowd and I lunching together. For a dummy, Elwood is one heck of a gentleman.

Many states are getting behind the adoption cause. Susan Allen, wife of Governor George Allen of Virginia and I pose with these great kids for a poster promoting adoption throughout the state.

I think every child deserves a home and love—don't you?

Lorraine and I together at the ground-breaking ceremony for the I. Lorraine Thomas Home for the Children's Home Society in South Florida.

Here I am speaking on the importance of adoption benefits for public employees at the National Governors' Association's 1994 winter meeting. South Carolina Governor Carroll Campbell (L) invited me to talk.

Chi Chi Rodriguez, Ray Floyd, and Jack Nicklaus: The winners of the 1993 Wendy's Three-Tour Challenge holding the check for the proceeds going to our adoption foundation. Hopefully, the real winners will be the children seeking adoption.

If we can help just one child get adopted, all our efforts will be worth it.

Isn't it great that these kids now have the chance to go to college? Sure is. The real breakthrough though—believe it or not—is in the planning. Although the Columbus Foundation gives generously to help the students, the real miracle comes from what businesspeople call *leverage*—before every dollar of foundation money that's used, more than *nine* other dollars are gotten from other organizations as scholarship support. It all comes from the planning that turns the idea of getting into college from a daydream into systematic, hard work . . . and then staying on top of every step for a year. Maybe two. But when you think about it, how is that different from anything else that's worthwhile in life?

Shouldn't every community have the motivation to create its own version of I Know I Can? If communities had that kind of program across the country, it would pull responsibility for funding college education down to the local level, which is where most of it should be anyway, and it would take it out of the hands of bureaucrats in Washington. Good news all around, the way I look at it. What ideas do *you* have for *your* community that can do the same thing? Come on! Be first! Won't it be great when others jump on your bandwagon?

SPURRING SUCCESS—THE SPITEFUL WAY. THE SPLENDID WAY.

A person without dreams can never be motivated. I sincerely believe that.

In the summer of 1944 I lost two jobs in less than a month. I was only twelve, but as I explain in *Dave's Way*, my adoptive father yelled at me that he doubted I would ever keep a job. That was a moment of truth for me. In what had been a not very classy life for me to begin with, this was an insult—a threat—that stung my self-respect as deeply as any message that had ever come my way. His words said I was going to live my life out as a worthless burden, and they hurt worse than any razor-strap whipping.

I vowed to prove him wrong. And I did.

From that day forward, I wanted role models, and I found them when I went to work for Frank and George Regas at the Regas Restaurant in Knoxville.

People who dined and worked there had dreams. We talked about and razzed each other over our dreams. "One day I'm going to own a whole *chain* of restaurants. Maybe three, maybe even four," I'd say.

"Aw, sure, Dave—tell us another one," my coworker might reply.

But plenty of people were dreaming back then. On Long Island, Bill Levitt, who started out building homes for defense workers during the war, was dreaming about huge housing complexes, like Levittown, that became the model for America's suburban subdivisions. In 1948, Kemmons Wilson in Memphis was dreaming about building his first motel, the flagship Holiday Inn.[1] The great scientist Enrico Fermi was dreaming about expanding the peaceful use of nuclear power and building reactors.

Sometimes the good side of someone serving your self-respect a challenge is that it causes you to dream hard and to dream smart. But turn it around. It may have been spite that motivated me, but inspiration can motivate just as easily. A magic phrase from a mom or dad or mentor can be the message that changes a life.

Mary Kay Ash once told me that, when she was just a salesperson with Stanley Home Products—and the most *un*successful one they had—she got up the gumption to tell the president of the company that she would be recognized as the *best* salesperson the following year. "He should have laughed," Mary Kay said, "but he didn't. He took my hand, looked me square in the eye, and said in a very kind voice, 'You know, somehow I think you will.'" She was, and then she

---

1. For an interesting discussion of both Levittown and Holiday Inn, see David Halberstam's *The Fifties*, (New York: Villard, 1993).

founded Mary Kay Cosmetics—a firm that has more women earning $50,000 to $100,000 a year than any company in the United States.

You know what I think can be one of the best motivators of all in the workplace? Fun. There's nothing wrong with a little kidding in the workplace. I'm not talking about reckless horseplay, but good, clean, harmless fun—kidding your workmates, but down deep still respecting them, like a family might do. There's too much pressure in jobs these days, and I don't think that people can deal with it without having a little fun with each other or poking fun at the organization. Work hard—you bet—but really motivated teams seem to remember the words to that old song: "In the meantime, in-between time, ain't we got fun?"

ELWOOD P. DOWD—SUPER DUMMY

Not long ago, I had lunch with Elwood P. Dowd. Cooked him up a bacon cheeseburger on the grill personally. But Elwood isn't much of an eater. Made a couple of comments to him about world affairs, but he said nothing back. And then I said some things to Elwood about business. Elwood just sat there; he's not much of a talker either.

In plain English, what Elwood is is a dummy—an honest-to-goodness dummy four feet tall, stuffed with rags. But he has a real nice smile. Elwood was stitched together by an elementary school teacher named Doug Hand at Thome Public School in Rock Falls, Illinois. Doug created Elwood when a parent of one of his students objected to the class reading *Pinocchio*. I wouldn't, because I think there's something to be learned from a puppet coming to life and having human dreams. Doug Hand thought there was a lesson there, too. So that was the making of Elwood; but don't think for a minute that Elwood just sits around all day.

He has shot hoops with Larry Bird. He met Kim Basinger

on Academy Awards night. He has been to Hungary and the NASA Space Center. Elwood's face flew on the space shuttle, too—about 3,500,00 miles. Elwood was a big hit in Washington. (In fact, he may have fit in there best of all.) We're seeing more of Elwood on national T.V. these days, too. Every place he goes, Elwood stops in for a photo opportunity. The photos go back to Doug Hand's fifth grade class in Rock Falls.

The kids plan whom Elwood will visit and what he is supposed to get out of the trip. Elwood visited me to learn what goes into making TV commercials. After Elwood's visit I sent a letter back to the kids at the elementary school to give them some encouragement. Doug is a real believer in teaching the three D's—Dreams, Desire, and Determination—along with the three R's. He's proof that anything is possible if you believe in yourself. I buy into that in a flash! And what about a hand for Mr. Hand, too? We spend so much time beating up on the work of schoolteachers these days, isn't it time we congratulate one who cooked up a nifty way to motivate kids?

Well done, Mr. Doug Hand and the dream-come-true youngsters of Thome Public School!

By the way, Elwood and I share some things in common. We're both hams I guess. We're both rags-to-riches stories, although Elwood is mostly rags. Still he's a sporty dresser: red sweater, blue jeans, and red-and-white beanie. I can understand why Kim Basinger took to him.

Praise And Perspective

One of the best ways to maintain your motivation is to not allow people's opinions about you to sidetrack you. For example, I don't think of myself as a celebrity, and I try to read very few articles written about me. Sometimes people who are publicized will read articles written about them and believe what's written. Then they will try to be the person the press says they are. Other celebrities will read articles about themselves and try to go out and prove that what's written is absolutely *not* true. Either way it's the same. Just be yourself, and you'll be much happier.

Not everybody gets his or her performance or comments reviewed in the newspapers or on television, but the same principle holds true for all of us. Inside yourself, you have to have a clear understanding of where you want to go and confidence in your ability to get there to always challenge what people may say about you.

Challenge the praise as well as the criticism. You have to listen to what your boss says about you. You also have to listen to what your husband or wife may say about you. Same goes for your father or your mother or your biggest customer or your biggest contributor. But successful people don't *over*listen. They listen with balance.

We're all human. The boss may pat you on the back because you really deserve it. Then again, the boss may be patting you on the back because he's read the weather report, and later today he's going to ask you to go to the airport to meet the president of the company in the middle of a rainstorm and chauffeur him back and forth to the construction site of a little supply depot sixty miles in the middle of the boondocks that the old man has been nagging to see. Your wife may tell you that your performance as a father is lacking, when it just could be that she's still sore about little Timmy spooning honey into the CD player yesterday while you were out swinging clubs on the driving range.

On the other hand, you can't look for a sniper behind every tree. Successful people are not cynics. You can't go marching around the world like a hard-core skeptic saying, "Sergeant Friday—Badge 714—Just the facts, ma'am." Not every compliment is phony; not every criticism is a trumped-up charge. That's why you need your own sense of clear direction and confidence about where you're headed.

A BUSLOAD CALLED DESIRE

To get people to believe astonishing things or to motivate them to do astonishing things, you have to bring them to the place where astonishing things happen. How many pilgrims have braved blazing sands and sailed stormy seas to see things firsthand, to check them out? No videotape, no second-hand account is ever as good as the real thing.

That's the way we looked at it when we first started selling franchises to operate Wendy's restaurants in a big way. We bought a great big MCI bus—which is really not a bus but a *motor coach*—and took interested people down the Ohio River to Memphis, starting in Columbus and passing through places like Dayton and Cincinnati. We sometimes started out with three prospects at first and then picked up a couple more at an airport they might fly into along the way—a few here and a few there. We would end up with as many as twenty when we hit the goal of our little trip, which was the Wendy's restaurant on Union Avenue in Memphis, run by Charlie Rodgers and Billy Plyler.

Charlie and Billy were (and are) quite a team. They started their careers in the commodities business working as traders. Then Charlie got an Arthur Treacher's franchise, and that's where I caught up with him. I was never too keen on how Charlie ran his Treacher's franchise (maybe it wasn't his fault), so I was skeptical at first about granting Charlie a Wendy's franchise. I wanted to make absolutely certain that he and his partner Billy could run a tight ship, so I handed them over to a couple of really tough operators in our company-owned stores with clear instructions to work these two guys until they dropped. I wanted them to work so hard that they could barely walk out of the restaurant at night.

They labored sixteen, seventeen hours a day, doing everything from chopping tomatoes to mopping floors. It must have worked, because they walked away from the experience with the greatest attitude that you could imagine. For their super show of energy and commitment, Charlie and Billy were awarded the Memphis market—and it quickly became a Wendy's showplace.

On our bus rides down to Memphis, I would tell people about the volume of business they would see—the number of people in the restaurant and the cars lined up through the parking lot and on to the street. Almost nobody believed me. I used to love to stand by the bus as they would get off gaping with wide-eyed stares on their faces. Could a restaurant really serve so many people, so fast? The folks on the bus would whistle through their teeth so loudly that it sounded like a teakettle convention had hit town. Me? I'd have a little "so-you-just-wouldn't-believe-me" smile on my face and would just nod my head a little.

Besides running a shipshape restaurant, Charlie and Billy were innovators. They shook up the structure—even at Wendy's. Here's how: The quick-service food industry was still pretty new. Everybody in it was thinking assembly line. They thought that being quick-service almost required you to have just one person specialized to do one thing, so it was nearly gospel in quick-service that there would be just one person working the grill and one person making the sandwiches. Why should it be, Charlie and Billy figured? If they had two people working the grill and two people making sandwiches, they could make a made-to-order hamburger sandwich faster without ruining its quality. They did it, and it worked. Then they added runners to go out to the cars and speed up taking orders. (These weren't like the runners of today who work with electronic headsets. These kids would actually run back and forth to and from the cars and the pick-up windows.)

I don't know all the reasons why Charlie and Billy became such great operators, but I think one was that they were the object of such attention. People say you're good, and you become even better. Even people who were already franchisees joined us on these trips, and they got better, too. Everyone's faith and conviction in our system grew, and that made the system itself stronger.

Today the lines are still long at the Memphis Wendy's because Charlie and Billy have remained focused on serving the highest quality food and providing the best quality service.

I'm not telling this story to brag about Wendy's. It's here to make a point about what a successful person has to do if they want to get an idea across. *Today, communication is the heart of success.* It all begins with pointing people in the direction of the right model. You can never short-change direct experience. I don't care if you need support for an orphanage, want to sell a producer on how well an audience reacts to the lines of a musical you wrote, or try to convince investors that your flower shop has the freshest roses in town. You have to give people real experience.

But, most of all, you have to know a communications tool when you see one. I own a much bigger motor coach now, but we no longer use it to sell franchises. I call it "Dave's Biggie Bus." It's forty-five feet long and has oversized blue leather chairs with footrests set up like a living room. There are five cellular phones aboard. The 450-horsepower engine is hooked up to a 110-gallon auxiliary fuel tank. The only thing we skimp on is the driver—since most of the time I drive it myself.

But this isn't a bus. It isn't really a motor coach either. It's a tool used to get communication across. It lets people share ideas. It lets them get comfortable with new ways of doing business. And it has allowed a lot of deals to happen. You or your group should have a communications tool, too. Yours doesn't have to cost a fortune. We may do our communicating inside my motor coach, but that's not the only way. I knew one fellow in Michigan who used his old Woody station wagon as a communication tool—driving buddies from the local restaurant association to see a perch-and-pike fish house down near Chicago that was doing a super job of serving customers.

Take a step back and consider: What is the "bus" that will make your dreams happen, that will help make you more successful? It doesn't have to be a business dream, either. Can that bus be your living-room parlor or a choir stall under the arches of a small country church? Do you know the people you have to gather together and to work with to achieve those dreams, and do you have some reason or drawing card that will bring them together? Most of all, do you have a clear and impressive dream that grabs—that draws—others to believe and to act?

YARDSTICKS

You can't motivate people for very long unless you measure them (and they measure themselves) against the right yardsticks. If you think there is only one way to measure success, you're going to shortchange yourself and other people, too. People tend to think there is really only one standard for every different thing that we do in life. For hockey, it's the Stanley Cup. For television shows, it's the Emmys. For being an entrepreneur, my friends tell me that it's getting the Horatio Alger Award.

But you can't take stock of success as simply as listing which award you might win. Lots of folks never see awards, yet are tremendously successful. In Ashley, a small town in northeastern Delaware Country, Ohio, I met a thirty-four-year-old paraplegic who lives life in a wheelchair. I asked this really friendly fellow—I'll call him Steve—what the word *success* meant for him.

Steve didn't miss a beat. It wasn't a second before he came out with the words, "Gravel path."

Say what?

Steve is a very bright guy; he was not spaced out on anything. He really meant "gravel path." Steve was a camper at a super place called Recreation Unlimited, the National Challenge Center for People with Disabilities, a 160-acre wooded and meadowed campus where physically and developmentally challenged people can go to vacation. Recreation Unlimited does a great job of asking its guests what they want to do and how they want to be treated.

Not long ago, we asked the campers if all the paths should be blacktopped; blacktop, of course, would be the easiest for people in wheelchairs to move around on. For Steve, being able to steer himself over a gravel path would be like a hefty rock climb for the rest of us. Don't blacktop everything, Steve and others like him said. Don't take our challenges away from us. So some of the paths are gravel, others are dirt (or mud when it rains), and others are blacktop.

At Recreation Unlimited, some of the guests who are blind or who are missing an arm or a leg can experience down-hill skiing in winter. Others choose to do less spectacular things such as track and field, cycling, boating, canoeing, or fishing. The biggest choice by far is camping. And that's a point to think about.

Twenty years ago we had one stereotype of challenged people. (Even the words that we use have changed. Kind people back then would call these folks "handicapped" while unkind people would call them "cripples.") The general view-point was that these people weren't going to do much of anything; that the best thing was just to store them away, to "warehouse them" where they would be the least trouble or out of sight.

Then our awareness started to change. You'd see people who had lost both legs race in marathons or somebody who was blind become a sharpshooter with a rifle just by using her ears to hone in on the target. On the one hand, this was great. On the other hand, it was bad. We tended to classify people with physical challenges as either (1) people who sat back and did nothing to overcome their disabilities *or* (2) people who did remarkable things. When we thought about people with disabilities, we thought about extremes. How little we under-stand about the motivation of most people with disabilities! The biggest group of all is actually the one in the middle—disabled people who are trying to do just a little bit better than they did yesterday, last week, or last year. There's a lesson here for us all.

When the guests of Recreation Unlimited were surveyed and asked about their favorite activity of all in the camp, they reported—as I said earlier—that it was camping, maybe in an "outpost" down near the lake. It could be that doesn't sound all that exciting to many people, but it's exciting to plenty of people with disabilities. It spells success for them.

Ninety-five percent of my day may go perfectly, but how often do I—and maybe you, too—write off the day as zero if one little thing goes wrong? Some of these special people chalk up a victory if they are able just to take a shower by themselves. All I can say is: What we take for granted in life!

I remember walking along the camp lake one evening and watching some mallard ducks skim along the water. Passing by a crackling campfire, I overheard some adult campers talking about how their lives were different from the lives of "normal" people. I don't think that they knew I was strolling by, but one of them used a phrase I don't think I'll ever forget to describe what I am, and what you probably are, too. He said it was hard sometimes to get the *"temporarily able-bodied"* people to understand the goals of challenged and disabled people.

Isn't that the truth? We start out life in a cradle, and many of us end up as invalids. Good health and the ability to get around are not something we can count on forever. We take being well for granted, and we live life like we'll be well forever.

Success. It's not really the neon lights and the publicity. More often, it's the small steps to make yourself stronger and to keep yourself well, measured against simple goals. Most of all, it's staying tuned to the truth that there are millions of yardsticks to measure life. Picking the right one at the right time could be one of the biggest clues to motivation that can ever be learned.

CREATIVITY

Creativity means change, but if you don't use common sense when you change things around, you are likely to end up further back than when you started. Not everybody can be creative. Accept it as a fact of life that if you aren't creative yourself, your challenge then becomes learning how to work with creative people.

Being creative doesn't always mean doing new things. Sometimes, it's using a creative idea that worked in one place and applying it to something totally different. I'm a disciple of reality. Successful creative dreams have to be realistic—within man's laws as well as God's—and within the realm of common sense.

What makes people creative? Sometimes, it's having your life shaken up. George Valassis is a pal of mine. For nineteen years he worked as an advertising salesman for his father's brother. One day his uncle decided to retire. His son, George's cousin, took over the business, and, well, he fired George. George had lost a comfortable, modest job, and he realized then and there that job security could vanish like a puff of smoke. He put his nineteen years of experience to use to come up with an innovative idea. He knew that advertisers like Procter and Gamble and General Foods were having a really tough time delivering coupons to customers quickly, so he came up with the idea of inserting a book filled with coupons into Sunday newspapers. To this day, when you open your Sunday paper and see that book of coupons inside, you're looking at what the ad industry calls a Valassis Insert. George sold the company he built for big bucks. If he hadn't gotten fired, would he have come up with this great idea? George doesn't think so. To this day, George says he just played the hand he was dealt. Pretty creative though, wasn't it?

THE THREE LADLE SCHOOL OF MARKET RESEARCH

I think that the highest sort of creativity is common sense creativity. It's not letting yourself get too fancy in how you see the world or in how you solve problems or in how you try out a new idea.

Our executive vice president of marketing at Wendy's, Charlie Rath, came up with something I call the Three Ladle School of Market Research. It all started when one of our executives wanted to launch a new product at Wendy's in the early '80s called a hot taco salad. The ingredients were chili, shredded lettuce, chopped tomato, chopped onion, grated cheese, and taco chips. The only item in the mixture that was not already a regular staple in our restaurants was the chips.

Well, this pretty good brainstorm—we later learned—got stuck somewhere in a maze of committees for darn near three months all because of too much caution. It came down to this, as everybody saw it with their thinking caps on: Were we or were we not going to spend $62,000 to bring in a crack squad of Harvard M.B.A. consultants to try out this new idea in three restaurants and to measure it to death with computers, legal pads, and graph paper over three weeks?

Maybe this would be a good idea, and sure, we had to test it. But was this the only way to run a test? Weren't we letting things get way out of hand and forgetting about using common sense to check up on a creative idea?

Now Charlie is a common-sense guy who's got creativity in aces, which is one reason he's so good, because it's hard to find people who are creative and have the discipline of common sense to boot. So Charlie wound up in the middle of the Great Taco Salad Stand-Off (which had nearly become a range war inside of Wendy's). He started by asking one simple question: "What pieces of equipment will we need in our restaurant kitchens to make this salad that we don't already have there?"

It turned out that all we were missing was a ladle that could scoop the chili out in the right quantity.

Did these ladles already exist? Sure enough they did.

How much did they cost? $12.39 apiece at the local restaurant-supply store. So that made $37.17 if we wanted to buy three.

How many taco chips would three restaurants need to run a test for three weeks? Oh, about $89 worth, wholesale. And if we took three headquarter's researchers and put them in stores for three weeks with survey forms to ask customers what they thought of the salad, how much would that cost—assuming the researchers were already on the payroll? Well, maybe $625 in expense money.

So for $751.17 in ladles, taco chips, and gas money—or $61,248.83 less than originally proposed by four dudes in three-piece suits handing out presentations in leather binders—and after just seventeen minutes of asking ourselves intelligent questions, we would now be able to find out if customers did or did not like the idea of buying a taco salad at Wendy's. Thanks to Charlie, that's how we did it. We tried. We studied. We learned. So that's why you see Taco Salad on the menu at Wendy's today, and our shareholders pocketed an extra sixty-one grand because we weren't dumb enough to get too smart checking out a good idea.

You can use this kind of common sense at home whenever you fiddle with a new idea:

- Are you about to pay for high-priced investment advice to manage a small mutual fund account when you could just wander down to the local public library and look at a couple of good business or consumer magazines?

- Are you thinking about buying a personal computer for your home through an expensive store rather than using the library again—or the advice of your son's best friend, who happens to be the greatest computer whiz since Mr. I.B.M.? (There was one of those guys, wasn't there?)

THE TRICK OF THE TRANSFER

Have I ever learned a lot writing books! There is something for which I may go down in publishing history: People tell me that I may be the first person to use fast-food tactics to sell books.

When I did the book tour for *Dave's Way*, I was autographing books at a big store in downtown Chicago, doing my best to spell people's names right and to put in the message they asked for. When I looked up, I was flattered—I mean I could have popped my buttons—to see such a long line, but I could also tell that the people were getting restless. Where had I had that feeling before? Then it dawned on me: I had seen frowns like that for decades as people waited in line to get their orders at restaurants.

So, what could we do about the long line? Why not use the same idea that we used at Wendy's? I asked one of the people helping me to take some file cards and to talk with the people in the line and to print the name they wanted me to write in the book, just like a Wendy's order taker marks down a customer's selection. That way I wouldn't be writing Steven for Stephen or Gene for Jean. If they wanted a special message, the helpers printed that out, too. People seemed to fidget less as they paid attention to getting their cards ready. I made fewer mistakes, and the line moved a whole lot faster. Simple solution, and it worked. Made-to-order, custom solutions usually do.

Our solution to the signature problem was to make a creative transfer, and it was nothing fancier than taking an idea that worked one way and putting it to use in a totally different way.

Another example of creative transfer may help get some kids adopted. We recently launched a statewide adoption poster campaign program in New Jersey. Most Wendy's in New Jersey now have a poster frame with space for the photographs of six children. These are youngsters available for adoption who have "special needs." They are older, physically or emotionally challenged, part of a sibling group, or minorities. As each child is adopted, his or her picture will be replaced by another youngster's picture. A few years back people started to show pictures of runaway or missing children on the backs of milk cartons to help track them down. That's where the adoption poster idea came from: we transferred a solution from there to here.

My hands-down winner for the creative transfer of the year is for the most sensible use of an answering machine I've ever heard of. When the national PTA picked their choice for the top educator in 1993, they chose Dr. Sharon Banks, principal of Northrop High, the biggest high school in northeast Indiana. One of the things that makes Sharon Banks so innovative is a setup she installed in the school called the Homework Hotline. The Homework Hotline is really just an answering machine. Each day the message is changed so that parents can pick up on what homework assignments their kids have each evening. When the recorded message is over, parents can then leave their own messages for teachers if they have questions about how youngsters are doing with a particular problem or a certain skill.

Simple thing like an answering machine. But instead of having it cluttered with unwanted messages it becomes a link between parents and teachers. What could be plainer or more sensible than that—but how many schools use it? Millions of homes in America have answering machines, but I bet that less than one percent of the schools do. Let's wake up and put some creative brains after the beep.[1]

Both of these are examples of how to put modern marketing to work for good causes. When we shoot a public service announcement for adoption, we work just as hard at making it be professional as when we shoot a commercial for Wendy's. Some people attack modern marketing and say it tries to twist the gears in people's minds. I think people are smarter than

---

1. Julia A. Van, "Award-Winning Principle Works Through Barriers to Involve Parents," *PTA Today*, September/October 1993, p.14.

that and prove it every day in how they shop. But if marketing can get next to their souls and consciences and get them to do some good, I say that's positive.

CREATIVE HOLES IN THE WALL

I love windows. Just love 'em. There are two ways customers get food for themselves at a restaurant. One is by walking through the door, and the other is by reaching up to a window. Wendy's was the first modern-day restaurant chain to do business out of a pick-up window. In the quick-service industry, windows are by far the fastest growing part of a restaurant's business. Everybody wants to grab a sack and cruise home to what Madison Avenue types call their cocoon, that cozy space within the walls of their own homes.

I want to tell you about the wonders and woes of restaurant windows—especially the woes—because it has to do with success. If you're going to be successful, you sometimes have to understand what's going on in the background. It has often been said that the railroads went bust because they thought they were in the train business and not the transportation business. It's true. The airlines put the railroads on ice. And how many acting careers have ended when the actor thought he was in the business of being a star instead of being an actor? How many senators have landed on the rocks after they became presidential hopefuls and stopped representing the people—the customers—in the state that elected them? How many marriages have gone south when the partners decided that they wanted to have it *all* instead of having it *right*?

You gotta know where your bread is buttered. And you have to know what can make it mold, too.

A Wendy's pick-up window is 4 feet wide by 3 feet high and sits 38 inches above the ground. Only two feet of the width actually slides open. Why only two feet? Because many city codes say that an opening of more than two feet can be unhealthy, as it can let in flies. Smart thinking.

Not paying attention to the size of a pick-up window can cause other problems, too. When one of our competitors tested adding pizza to their menu, they tried it out first as an item served over the counter. People liked it. The chain decided to expand the test and made the product available through pick-up windows. What they soon learned was that they couldn't get the pizza box through the pick-up window horizontally. When the box was tilted to make it fit, the pizza turned into a glob. So, do you change the pizza, change the box, or change thousands of windows? The problem had nothing to do with the food. It was a snag caused by packaging not fitting through a window.

What is the most difficult thing to get through the two feet of a pick-up window? It isn't a cup of coffee or a baked potato. It's not a bowl of chili or even a pizza box that's too big for the opening.

It's information.

The first Wendy's window had a hospital intercom system. I can still remember some joker testing it out with, "Calling Dr. Dave, calling Dr. Dave, report immediately to refrigeration!" The system was plenty better than the intercoms you'd find in the old-style drive-ins—those were really caveman stuff. Today our order-takers inside have electronic headsets, and the outside microphones are packed in foam-filled cubes. The circuits are wired to filter out the highs and lows (car and outside noise) and to pick up just the sounds of human voices. Still, even today things work a lot better when somebody drives up in a Mercedes or a Lexus than when somebody comes through in an old jalopy that needs a valve job and and a new muffler.

A young lady might pull up to a pick-up window and say, "Single cheese, no onion." Somebody drops a tire iron in the parking lot at exactly the wrong time, and all the order-taker hears is "Single cheese,—onion." Ten minutes later we can have a very unhappy customer. And another thing has happened that many of us don't realize. With the continuing wave of immigration to America, it's much harder to understand all the accents that might be heard in a single day. It's wonderful that all these different people think America is such a great place to live, because it is. But there are Wendy's restaurants in New York or California where you'll hear English with an Albanian accent, English with a Haitian accent, English with a Sikh accent—on and on—all within minutes. How some of our order-takers, do it, I don't know. I'm still struggling to understand people who speak English with an English accent!

The pick-up window is a hole in the wall with great opportunity—we think that windows in most of our mature restaurants can do a million dollars worth of sales a year—but we still have problems to fix. Believe me, one thing I would love to see at a Wendy's pick-up window is a canopy, but the industry has found that canopies just don't work. No matter how many signs or cautions were posted about clearance or not bumping into support beams, restaurant operators were forever finding that customers would run their cars into the canopy. We used to call the favorite maneuver the "two-step" because the customer would first ram the car's right front fender into the support beam and then back the left rear fender into the building trying to make up for the first mistake. Bottom line: no canopies! But there is another problem we think we know how we're going to fix.

The idea started one day when our data processing vice president Glenn Barr went to Ohio Stadium to see the Buckeyes play football against the University of Washington. The big, fancy scoreboards in stadiums these days can do nearly anything but win the game for the home team. More and more of them are used to communicate emergency messages when someone has to be paged at the game. It was a brilliant, sunny day in Columbus that Glenn was at the game, and he picked up on something else. Despite the sun's brilliance, you could still see messages on the board because of the way the scoreboard was lit. Nothing was washed out, nothing glared.

This got Glenn to thinking. A major reason why stadium scoreboards are designed to do what they do is that they have to get information across when everybody is yelling, cheering, and stamping their feet. Wasn't this the same type of problem you have in a restaurant drive-through—getting accurate information across when the background sound is less than perfect?

Glenn turned the project over to a bright computer programmer by the name of Chak Pang and his team, and they came up with an idea called the Scoreboard. Now when customers put in orders over the speaker, they see an automatic readout of what they ordered and the price on a screen right in front of their eyes before they move to the pick-up window to get their food. The accuracy of the orders with the Scoreboard is testing out more than ninety percent! People who are hard of hearing find the Scoreboard an extra plus because now they can see their order instead of having to strain to hear it. By 1995 most of the company-owned Wendy's will have Scoreboards.

One reason people take to the Scoreboard so easily—I'm sure—is that everybody is used to reading computer screens nowadays. (The Scoreboard is really just a computer display hooked up to the order-taker's cash register inside.) Because the Scoreboard makes things so much clearer, customers move through the drive-through faster, and that's another plus.

There you have it. Most people I've met outside the food industry—and some inside—think that the biggest challenge in managing a pick-up window is what food you're going to serve. If you haven't beat that problem before you put the hole in the wall, you're lookin' at the wrong end of the horse. Getting on top of communication and weather is just as important. The lesson: Improving the quality of the food would have had nothing to do with making the pick-up window a better success. Even though food was the main reason people were coming to the pick-up window, our ability to execute—to make using the window itself more accurate, faster, and less of a hassle—is the way that we improved its success.

That's what I call being creative.

LEADERSHIP

Everybody is saying that we need to stop putting leaders on pedestals. I'm not so sure. The real problem is finding leaders who truly deserve to keep their pedestals. What knocks off more leaders than anything else is when they preach something and then don't practice it. Of all the kinds of things leaders are supposed to do, none is more important than setting an example. Ben Franklin had it right when he wrote in Poor Richard's Almanac, "Well done is better than well said." I don't think we should do away with pedestals altogether, though. In fact, I think we ought to be putting a lot more "little people"—people who have really achieved something— on pedestals so that ordinary folks have a better, clearer idea of who's doing the job and who's setting the pace.

J. B. Fuqua is a titan of industry who built a huge conglomerate and broadcast empire. J. B. is also a guy who still knows the meaning of being humble. Born to a poor family, his grandparents adopted him when he was two months old after his mother died.

When J. B. was out on his own and wanted to learn about radio electronics, the only library he knew about to borrow books from was Duke University's. They loaned him the books. It wasn't a bad deal for Duke: after J. B. hit the bullseye in his own companies, he has since invested $15 million in the Duke University business school, helping put it in the front ranks of all the business schools in the U.S.

First and foremost, J. B. is a leader. In addition to the donations he's given Duke, he's donated $4 million to train managers in Russia and Ukraine as these nations put true free enterprise into practice. And then there's the $10 million that he's giving to Prince Edward County, Virginia, to help turn around the educational system for youngsters in kindergarten through twelfth grade. It will be a model of doing the right thing for rural school systems throughout the United States.

It's not the money that makes J. B. successful as a leader. It's the fact that he won't let go. J. B. will tell you that leadership doesn't stop with giving, but begins there. He's in his seventies, yet you'll find him all over—at Duke, in Farmville, in Virginia, or over in Kiev—out there giving his leadership to others, passing on his own experience and wisdom.

J. B.'s style is real leadership—letting go in the doing, but not letting go in the guiding.

THE WIN-WIN WOMAN

Pam Masters has come a long way from running a little homecookin' restaurant in downtown Louisville, Kentucky, and driving a UPS truck. Today she's a dynamic community pacesetter in South Florida. Even so, Pam would be the first to tell you that she didn't go it alone, and that she was lucky to have had several good mentors along the way.

Pam has a gift for talking to youngsters. One of her strongest messages is that good habits are really important but that they don't mean a lick if you don't have good values, too.

Take drug dealers, for instance. "Drug dealers have a plan," she says. "And they're organized, too—how else could they keep coming around at certain times and keep track of all their 'accounts'? And drug dealers have tremendous self-discipline. They will stay up all night and keep coming back over and over again to get your 'business.' They're into customer service, big time. But there is one thing that drug dealers don't have: values. Do they care if the drugs kill you? No, they could care less about anything except for your money and their power!

"Why do values matter so much? Having good values is the one thing in this world that will let you sit in a rocking chair on your front porch when you get old and watch your grandkids with a smile on your face. You have a choice: you can go for the fast buck and end up lonely, unhappy, or even dead, or you can tackle life the right way—no short cuts. You've got to pay your dues; it's part of the process. Start today with good habits and *true* success will be yours tomorrow!"

America should be producing generation after generation of proud citizens. I mean, that's our job. And people like Pam Masters make sure we do it right. Pam believes in contagious goodness—which is why I call her the Win-Win Woman. If there isn't a benefit to both sides, it isn't a good deal. Using that formula, she has programs piled on top of programs that have led to many good things being done.

Today, Pam is the guiding force behind Enterprise Ambassador, a breakthrough program teaching leadership to youngsters. Each year Juniors from Broward County's public and private high schools are selected through written applications and personal interviews by businesspeople from the local chambers of commerce to be part of the program. These kids have what Pam calls a "spark." They don't necessarily have the best grades, but they do have an interest in business and desire to succeed. Each class winds up with a great mix of kids with all kinds of skills and backgrounds. Isn't that the way it works in the real world anyway?

Enterprise Ambassador teaches the "big picture" of business through a summer institute, provides hands-on experience by pairing each student with a personal business mentor, gives seminars on personal and basic business skills, and encourages social responsibility through community service projects. More often, it's the community service projects—most targeted at helping pre-teens—that show the character and commitment of these young people. They say the proof is in the puddin' and there are already success stories about some of the Ambassadors. Let me tell you about a few.

Both President Bush and President Clinton have acknowledged Tasha Joseph for her works with Embrace-A-Child. Tasha was only seventeen when she started to organize high-school groups to partner up with neighborhood children's centers. Tasha herself learned the ropes of juggling fund-raising, running day-to-day operations, and putting together a six-week summer camp. Tasha is still committed to Embrace-A-Child while finishing her last year as an international business major at Florida International University.

Chad Perlyn, now a Northwestern University senior headed for medical school, is another Enterprise Ambassador success. Chad created a program called Doc Adopt because he knew poor children didn't have the same high quality medical care that his parents could afford for him. Doc Adopt is a referral service—really a match-maker—that tries to get physicians to "adopt" a disadvantaged child in the community and to give that youngster medical care. The local medical association greeted the idea with open arms.

Chad's younger brother, Eric, wasn't to be outdone. His brainchild is called Stepp'n Up, a program that puts shoes on the feet of needy kids every year during the holidays. So far, Eric has been responsible for over six hundred pairs of new shoes going to disadvantaged children.

The Ambassador Program's mentors—and they include some of the highest-powered movers and shakers of the Ft. Lauderdale community—find that the kids are just great to be around. They're provocative and fresh and have actually caused some of the mentors to question some practices that they have in their own organizations. "By the way," these mega-buck bosses will sometimes scratch their heads and ask, "just why *do* we do it that way?"

As the kids grow older, some of their Enterprise Ambassador Program experiences sink in as they see something in later life or take a formal college course on a certain subject. One Ambassador explains that light bulbs are always going off in his head as he understands why something he first learned in Enterprise Ambassadors is relevant.

There's something we often forget about leadership—we forget how to bridge the connection from the real success stories of today to the likely success stories of tomorrow. Sure, the business schools and the fancy seminars and corporate internships all have their place. But what about *little* people with *big* ideas getting together with bigger people with big ideas and doing something for the community? Why shouldn't that work, too?

Well done, Pam Masters, and all the leaders with you and coming up beside you, for telling us where to go and the way to get there!

How I Got My M.B.A. Before My G.E.D.

I dropped out of high school when I was fifteen because I couldn't handle working such long hours and going to school at the same time. I was on my own, living at the "Y," and afraid of being broke. It was dumb to drop out, and it made life a lot harder for me in a lot of ways. Yet, even though I left school, I ended up what many people would call a leader. Responsible leaders have to be careful about what they do and how they talk about their mistakes.

Setting an example is what leadership is all about. Going back to get my G.E.D. degree was leading by example. Students kept asking me: Why didn't *I* go back and get my G.E.D.? Wasn't I supposed to be a mentor after all? I needed to get my G.E.D. in order to go on speaking to high-school students. Here I was, talk after talk, telling kids not to drop out of school or to go back to school. But what about me? Why was my case different from anybody else's?

When I told Lorraine I wanted to get my G.E.D., she just said do it. I had to take a lot of tests, about six hours worth. A tutor helped me prepare. I was tired of being called a dropout, and I finally did something about it. That G.E.D. certificate is framed and holds a place of honor in the hallway of our Florida home.

Coconut Creek High School, outside Ft. Lauderdale, adopted me. I was voted most likely to succeed by our graduating class of 1993. Lorraine and I went to the prom (we were named honorary king and queen), and I'll never forget the lead accordion player, who was wearing Buddy Holly glasses, letting loose with "Let's Go to the Hop" one more time on his gold-glittered Wurlitzer. Before we went to the prom that night, my son Kenny called me and told me to have a good time but to be home by ten. Wiseguy—just like his old man.

Don't get the idea that I'm the biggest cheese to ever go back to school. Alicia Villanueva dropped out in the eighth grade, but she went back to school. Today she teaches ESL

(English as a second language) and the National PTA has given her its highest honor, the Hearst Award for Outstanding Teaching. Alicia Villanueva is the pride of Salinas, California.[1] Think about what she achieved. If you drop out of school, you may slam the door on many opportunities; but don't let yourself think that door can't be reopened or that you'll never go back. It may be tougher to go back later and it may be a lot smarter to do it right the first time, but you can always go back to school. The only real learning disability is believing that you can't do any more learning.

I got my M.B.A. long before my G.E.D.; I even have a photograph of me in my M.B.A. graduation outfit—a snazzy knee-length work apron. I guarantee you that I'm the only founder among America's big companies whose picture in the corporate annual report shows him wielding a mop and a plastic bucket. That wasn't a gag; it was a case of leading by example.

At Wendy's, M.B.A. does not mean Master of Business Administration. It means Mop Bucket Attitude. It's how we define satisfying the customer through cleanliness, quality food, friendly service, and atmosphere. Some people may think that computer printouts should come first in business, but as I see it, everything in a restaurant had better start with a clean floor. So mopping floors is not some dirty job to avoid. It's one of the most important jobs in the restaurant, and we should pay serious attention to it.

As we say at Wendy's, you build a business one customer at a time. Make customers and quality number one on your list. If you think of your customers, or business locations, as just numbers, you'll be out of business in no time. Any M.B.A. knows that—at least, any Wendy's M.B.A. does.

---

1. Meletta Cutright, "1986 Hearst Award Goes to a Truly Outstanding Teacher," *PTA Today*, Oct. 1986, pp. 7–8.

Martha's G.E.D. Army

"I want *YOU* to join Martha's G.E.D. Army."

That's what the sign said; only the picture on the poster wasn't a guy with a striped top-hat and a beard, but a determined woman in a WAC uniform. That woman was Martha Wilkinson, wife of Kentucky's 53rd governor, Wallace Wilkinson. Martha was the general of what was to become Kentucky's G.E.D. Army.

Both Martha and Wallace were born and raised in rural Casey County, Kentucky. It's no Park Avenue or Palm Springs; in fact, the locals often say that "the only opportunity is somewhere else." The warm roots of a loving family and friends and the character-building disciplines of a rural upbringing are great benefits, but Martha knew there was more. And the most important "more" was the need for quality education. Out of frustration with the lack of opportunity, or out of the need to help support their families, far too many young people in Casey County and other counties like it often drifted away from school.

In high school, the freshman class of 1959 started nearly one-hundred fifty students strong. Four years later only a third remained; Martha, Wallace, and 52 others. Twenty-eight years later, when the Wilkinsons moved into the governor's mansion, Casey County was still leading the nation in the percentage of adults without a high school diploma or G.E.D. Half of the adults in the region had dropped out of high school. Martha knew what her personal mission as Kentucky's first lady would be and she opened up the throttle, building awareness everywhere she could.

In August, 1988, Martha started her G.E.D. offensive rolling at the Kentucky State Fair. She let people know about Kentucky's great "G.E.D. on T.V." series, produced by the state's educational television network and used all over the U.S. (Kentucky is one of the few states where students can enroll in a formal G.E.D. program and take classes over educational television.) From posters and billboards and television screens across the state, a crisp-collared Martha Wilkinson fired up Kentucky's undereducated adults with the ol' familiar challenge, "I want you in my Army."

Thousands answered the call. Within just a few months, the number of people in G.E.D. programs soared. That included people on the "inside" too: the state Corrections Cabinet reported a fifty-five percent increase in inmates going after a G.E.D., and at least some hope of a future.

The whole deal turned infectious. At a benefit concert sponsored by Fruit of the Loom (Kentucky's largest manufacturing employer) in 1989, country-music artist Waylon Jennings was moved to tell the crowd that he had always regretted not completing high school. At another concert the next evening, Martha met Waylon backstage and gave him a set of the "G.E.D. on T.V." tapes. Waylon vowed he would complete the program.

Waylon's commitment turned plenty of others on to "The Big E." Everyone could relate to his studying on the bus, getting tutored by his young son Shooter, and scratching his head about fractions. I sure could. While I was studying for my own G.E.D., many is the time I wanted to dial up one of my kids and ask them a "trick question" from my homework, but I just bit into my eraser. I guess I've gotten soft over the years.

On January 29, 1990, Martha handed Waylon his G.E.D. certificate at a special ceremony in Frankfort. During a G.E.D. telethon that night, the two of them encouraged people to enroll. And people believed. The phone company logged over 107,000 telethon calls in response.

Waylon's success story is only one of thousands. Later, Martha's Army took their message into the schools and passed out copies of the Kentucky author Jesse Stuart's *The Beatinest Boy* to each of the state's 50,000 sixth graders. Printed on the back cover of each copy was a message to the kids to stay in school and to encourage their moms and dads to get their G.E.D.s.

Why did Martha's Kentucky G.E.D. campaign work? I can think of four reasons why:

- She picked a cause to which she was personally committed. She never forgot where she came from and she knew the problems firsthand. It's no surprise that she was so convincing.

- Martha spoke to people in a way they could understand. From the Uncle-Sam style poster to recruiting Waylon Jennings, people were able to get the message quickly.

- This campaign turned the so-called "idiot box" into a "brain box." TV was used to publicize the need for people to get their G.E.D.s, and the "G.E.D. on T.V." series was made available to many more people as a result.

- Kids were asked to help get their parents excited about education. Let's not forget the power of the "littlest role model." I can remember a little baby in a Bethlehem manger who started changing the world from the very day he was born.

Well done, General Martha! We hope that this program marches forward into every state.

WE NEED PEDESTALS—22,000 OF THEM, I'D SAY

Anybody who enjoys sports—certainly everybody who likes college football—would recognize the Heisman Trophy. This bronze statue is a little more than a foot high, weighs about twenty-five pounds and shows a straight-arming, side-stepping football player. The Heisman Trophy winner is the personal success story in college athletics each year, and winning it is a real distinction. It's awarded each year by the Downtown Athletic Club of New York City to the most outstanding college football player in the country. The first player to receive it was Jay "One-Man Gang" Berwanger of the University of Chicago in 1935. In 1993 the winner was Charlie Ward of Florida State. Other names of Heisman winners are a knock-your-socks-off roster of star athletes—players like Paul Hornung, Roger Staubach, and Tony Dorsett.

We all know the Heisman winners, but who the heck was Heisman himself?

John Heisman was one of the most successful college coaches in history. He died back in 1936, but he still stands among the top twenty in all-time victories. He coached in a bunch of different schools, but his biggest successes were at Georgia Tech where he led the team to three unbeaten seasons.

You know what I like most about John Heisman? He was an innovator. He was the first to have the center snap the ball between his legs, which sure cut down on fumbles; and he was one of the first, if not the first, to come up with the break-through of the forward pass. That's why it comes as no surprise that Heisman Trophy winners in the sixty years since his death have often added some new style or new standard to the game of college football.

It's a special honor for me that I've gotten to know the player who many think is the greatest Heisman Trophy winner of all time. He's the only person to win the trophy twice, and his name is Archie Griffin. Archie was a halfback who really helped change the basics of the running game in football. Before his time, the great runners were mostly dancers; they would tease the defense and flash a little leg, then dodge or pivot out of the way before a tackler would pounce on them. Archie was different. He wasn't that big or that fast, but he knew how to run as part of the team. He built a real bond with blockers. Because of it, they would hold their blocks for maybe just a half-second longer. And that half-second was enough to push the ball forward.

Archie, who is today a member of the executive staff of his alma mater Ohio State's athletic department, is one of the most low-key guys I know. He doesn't spout off about winning the Heisman twice. In fact, it's hard to get him to say much about ever winning the Heisman at all. He told me once, "I felt that me winning the Heisman reflected the success of our team as a whole. . . . In 1974, when I won the Heisman, it was as if the whole team won the Heisman because they did just an outstanding job and I was just surrounded by some great athletes."

Archie admits that the Heisman opened a lot of doors for him, but it also has been a big responsibility. A Heisman winner really has something to live up to.

When Archie is asked to speak to youngsters in schools today, he tells them that what gave him the chance to win the Heisman were the values he learned as a young boy growing up in Columbus, Ohio. He put it this way: "What helped me most were the priorities my parents gave us to live by. There were eight children—including six brothers and a sister, and my father certainly wanted his kids disciplined. Next, my junior high-school guidance counselor made a huge impact on my life with what he called the Three D's: Desire, Dedication, and Determination. I think that a real leader has to be disciplined and will probably want discipline from the people they're leading. That certainly included my high-school coach, Coach Woody Hayes at Ohio State, and even a couple of pro coaches I played for."

Last year some of us at Wendy's got to thinking about how we might spread the Archie Attitude. The idea that we came up with was the Wendy's High School Heisman Award. It's based on the college Heisman with a few extra twists to it.

First of all, we wanted every high-school student in the United States to be eligible to win the award. That meant that girls could compete along with boys. Second, we felt that the award should have three measures: scholastic achievement, athletic excellence, and good citizenship. This is the best part of the High School Heisman—and the part that I think John Heisman would have liked too, since he was keen on innovation—because it means that any winner has to have balance.

He or she has to be good across the board and has to know how to juggle achievement in all three key skills that schools teach. There are six Heisman regions across the country for the run-off competitions. Regional winners and runners-up from these six regions earn trophies and cash grants for their schools. There are about 22,000 high schools in America, and the principals of those schools will have the chance to nominate their school's entrants. The first award will be given out in December 1994, the same time as the college Heisman Trophy.

The trophies and grants are nice, but they aren't the real heart of the program. Through the High School Heisman we in the community and in the school system have the chance to point to 22,000 role models for young people in America—22,000 young scholar-athlete-citizens who have learned discipline and who represent what's right in America. Archie Griffin is going to chair the program, and recently he said to me, "You know that's wonderful, because 22,000 kids can make a huge impact on a lot of people."

Well done, Archie Griffin!

Every night we see those awful news reports about guns in schools, drugs on street corners, and teen pregnancies. When I was growing up, I think that more things were done to recognize the kind of behavior we think is good; you know, Eagle Scouts and honor rolls and all the rest. Now much of this has fallen out of favor. People—especially some know-it-all social scientists—think it's wrong to call attention to kids who are doing the right thing, because it may give other kids an inferiority complex. I'm pretty sure that if some of these psychological social workers had played around in my head when I was a kid, my gray cells might have ended up in a jar in some medical school rather than being used to amount to anything.

Let's recognize young people who are doing things right!

PART FOUR

ONWARD: PUTTING YOURSELF SECOND AND OTHERS FIRST

If going upward and reaching for excellence is where success gets tricky, going onward by putting yourself second and others first is where success really gets tough. Most books on success tell you that you have arrived when you cross the finish line first. I believe that really successful people are happy with being in the back seat, and that they would like to help many others get there first.

People who make this last big success step, I think, really have three things down cold: Genuine responsibility, courage, and generosity. Onward is the direction Success Soldiers strive toward—Christian or any other kind.

RESPONSIBILITY

It was a real temptation to write about responsibility back in the first section of this book along with the first steps of getting your own act together. But I dodged that idea because it would be taking responsibility too lightly. We try to teach children responsibility, and that's good, but most people don't get the full meaning of responsibility until they are older and have gained solid experience, made some decisions, and learned from their mistakes—not simple mistakes "following orders," but mistakes when you're trying to do something really tough or when you're trying to excel. Making those sorts of mistakes teaches a human being judgment and helps toughen a person's backbone, too.

Mature responsibility also means realizing that no one person can be responsible for everything and that you can't be successful if you are stumbling around juggling the whole world on your shoulders. Responsible people take tough stands against shortcuts and have their antennae up all the time because they know the temptation to take an "easy street" shortcut is always available.

Responsible people make sure that other people with duties act responsibly, too; like when taxpayers hold politicians accountable for getting the business of government done.

Last of all, successful people have the responsibility to use whatever recognition or honor they may have earned for themselves on behalf of good causes. Instead of stealing the limelight, they build awareness by allowing a good cause to soak up the attention.

169

My son Kenny says that the most important piece of advice I ever gave him came in 1979 as the two of us were driving over the Oakland Park Bridge in Ft. Lauderdale. He was thinking about becoming a Wendy's franchisee. I gave him my opinion, which was not to do it. I didn't come out and say why, but my feeling was that he wasn't ready for that kind of responsibility—and I guess down deep I didn't want to see him fail. That's what I was thinking; but when he told me his mind was made up, I just said, "Don't ever forget how you got here, and don't ever let yourself become complacent." Kenny went on to become pretty successful in the restaurant business, and now he's cooking up a deal to barter American chicken feet and other American-made products over in China. (Don't laugh, in some parts of China, people will take a chicken foot over a chicken sandwich any day!) Kenny says my advice really helped him. I don't know. I think I may have talked too much that day, because everything I had to say could have been summed up in just two words: Be responsible.

MY THREE MOST SUCCESSFUL MISTAKES???

Admitting your mistakes is a key part of responsibility. I've made plenty of mistakes in my life, and I want to talk about three really outstanding ones. The first I made when I was playing in the little leagues. The second one almost prevented me from being called up to the major leagues of business. And the third was definitely an All Star air ball.

Mistake Number One: I dropped out of school. It wasn't until I turned sixty that I fixed that problem. For four decades, I put myself at an awful disadvantage in the business world and in so many other parts of life, too. People used to say, "Look at what Dave Thomas achieved, and he didn't even graduate from high school." They meant well when they said it, but it always bothered me when someone made a point of it—especially if it was a youngster—because some people used whatever success I had as a good excuse for not finishing school themselves. The way I've looked at it is, "What more could Dave Thomas have achieved in his life if he finished high school on schedule and maybe even went on to college in night school?"

Mistake Number Two: I smugly rested on my laurels after Wendy's initial success. Right after we got Wendy's going, I figured it would be clear sailing for a small local business. I was too much of a knucklehead to notice that there would be big pressure to grow this successful little business. I should have been planning ahead, worrying about the next step rather than being smug about my success.

Mistake Number Three: I built a large, glamorous office building. When Wendy's made it big and was listed on the New York Exchange, hadn't Wendy's earned the right to a huge, gorgeous headquarters? That was envy—envy of the world of big corporations, and envy can be a very expensive sin as far as buildings are concerned. We soon learned this as I paid for the real estate, the building and maintenance costs, and for loads of people that other managers wanted for their departments.

Mistakes make the woman or the man. I really believe that. And each of these three mistakes was a doozie.

Each mistake taught me a new way to come back from the mistake that I had made. From this guy's angle, mistakes are the starting point for the best learning in life.

What were the lessons I learned?

- Because I was a dropout, I learned what it meant to work hard very early in life. Dropouts are unacceptable in society; people look down on them. It didn't take me long to learn that dropouts had to work harder just to get by and superhard to break through. Later on, because I was tired of being called a dropout, I was able to go back and get my G.E.D. when I was a senior citizen. People tell me that what I've done is inspiring others. I don't know if that's so, but if it is, then all the better.

- Because I sat on my laurels and ignored my problems, I didn't prepare for the future expansion of the business and found myself chasing my tail for years to come. Not looking for problems is a problem itself. You heard me right, although it may sound silly to say so. People who ignore problems can't change or grow. Now I snoop around for problems to turn them into growth opportunities.

- Because we built a huge headquarters—our own super-duper Tower of Babel, we added too much staff, building up our expenses—and we actually hurt our ability to talk with each other and make sense, just like the folks in old Babylonia. This may be the most complicated lesson I've learned. Afterwards we refused to let our staff grow as our number of restaurants grew. In fact, as turnover has happened over the years, we have let the staff shrink in some areas to a fraction of what it once was. It's a hard lesson to learn, but the size of an organization should never be allowed to grow too fast, no matter how rosey the future may look.

So, I've goofed up and come out okay so far. That's not to say that I didn't come out scared to the bone sometimes, resolving that I wouldn't make the same mistake twice. All in all, my take, I guess, is that mistakes are usually deadly only if you don't follow up on them, change your way of living, and learn to do things more responsibly.

THE CAROL STORY STORY

I've been on *CBS This Morning* a couple of times and have gotten to know a swell producer there by the name of Carol Story, which is a great last name to have if you happen to be in the news business.

Carol and her husband are really nice people, and Carol is known as one of the best producers in the business, but they are a pair of tough cookies, too. They have the guts to do things that definitely are not easy. You see, they adopted a fourteen-year-old girl, and they did it through a public agency.

As a friend of Carol's puts it, there's a reason God made puppies and kittens so cute: Not many people want to take over care of a full-grown dog or cat. Maybe the same thing is true for human beings. Many people who consider adoption are out after what experts call the "Gerber baby"—healthy, cute as a calendar pin-up, and hassle-free. Fresh off the assembly line, minus the stretch marks and nine months of morning sickness. With a teenager, however, character, personality, and values are already there.

Carol Story is a real straight talker, and she has some great tips for people considering adopting an older child. The way I see it, if people knew exactly how to deal with what they were up against, more people *would* adopt older youngsters.

Let me spell out some of Carol's ideas, and I think you'll see why they seem pretty sensible to me:

- When you adopt an older child, there will be things you can't control and things you can't change. Accept it—this young person is coming to you with certain attitudes and habits that just won't change. You didn't get to lay the foundations. If a kid is adopted at the age of twelve and then runs away or gets in trouble at school at age sixteen, the real reason things go wrong may be because of what happened when he or she was only five, or even in the cradle. Carol says that adopting an older child is more like getting married than having a baby. There's plenty of truth to that.

- Save your battles for the important things. Carol's daughter was fourteen when she was adopted. After dinner on her first day in high school, their new daughter announced she was taking off for the mall to hang out with friends. Carol said no way, this was a school night. You do homework, you spend a little time on the phone—that's it. Her new daughter was bowled over. "How dare you tell me how to spend my free time? I've been hanging out until ten at night in the parking lot of the 7–11 since I was six!" All Carol said was, "Young lady, I don't know who let you do that, but the rules in this home are different." The law was laid down on the basics, and that's the way it should be.

- Be fair but firm regarding the "other" parents. Biological parents have rights, but adoptive parents have rights, too. Practical tips: Biological parents can call if they want to, but not too often. For example, every night is too often, but once every six weeks, on birthdays, and on Christmas—sure. They can write any time, of course (writing is work and most people don't want to do it). Otherwise, kids will go "parent shopping" and pit biological parents against adoptive parents. Sometimes even former foster parents get in the act—especially if they were attached to the adopted youngster. Remember the commandment, "Thou shalt have no other gods before me" (Exodus 20:3). The same thing is roughly true for parents: In a healthy home, you can have only one set of parents calling the shots at any one time.

Carol says that adopting her daughter, who's now nearly thirty, married, and with kids of her own, was the best thing she ever did. Carol and her daughter are as close as you can imagine, and her daughter's values are as true and as strong as Carol's own.

As I heard the Carol Story story, the one thing that really stood out for me was how responsible these parents were in doing what they did. They also knew what they were responsible for and what they weren't. Many people lose sight of that.

Carol is Irish to begin with and can talk a good piece anyway, but get her started about her daughter like I did the last time I was in New York and there's no stopping her. Finally, I had to say, "Carol, we have a show to do. . . ." I'm the interviewee, she's the producer, and I'm reminding her that we have a show to do. But when you're really proud about something, priorities just get mixed up, I guess.

EASY STREET IS CLOSED FOR REPAIRS

Wendy's didn't start franchising until 1973, and even then I was hesitant to sell franchises because I had been a franchisee of Kentucky Fried Chicken. In the late sixties, the franchising industry was in its infancy. It didn't understand how to give service to franchisees. And it wasn't doing a very good job in general.

Many franchisors wanted to do things too simply. I'm all for simplicity, but you can't just put the patty on the grill and walk away from it. It's not going to cook itself; you have to work it and stay with it. You have to make a commitment to make every sandwich. Neither can you do it a certain way for two years and then find a simpler way to do it once you're a big business. I like to put it this way: *Easy street is closed for repairs.*

Whenever anyone mentions to me that he or she has a shortcut, I always ask, "Okay, but if we don't do it that way, what's the *long*cut instead?" I've always remembered my Grandma Minnie's regular advice to me, "Don't cut corners, boy!"

Here's what generally goes into a shortcut, regardless of whether you're in the food industry or not:

- Cheating on the time you need to get a quality result.

- Working with cheaper parts or ingredients which may be preassembled or come from lower-quality sources.

- Focusing on the ends versus the means—as in ringing the cash register short-term instead of building long-term loyal customers.

- Reducing the number of choices your customers have just to make things easier for yourself.

- Beating out a competitor or rival by using some unfair advantage such as an unforeseen, uncontrollable crisis against them.

I hate to boast about Wendy's being the long-cut alternative in the quick-service restaurant business, but I truly think we are: We cook every hamburger almost four minutes and at the right temperature. (We also learned how to make each sandwich in fifteen seconds. The trick is to always have hamburgers cooking when customers come into the restaurant.) We use only fresh quality ingredients. We put customer satisfaction first. We give our customers choices. And we try to compete as fairly as we can.

In the quick-service business, Wendy's has the leading reputation for quality. That means we would also have the most to lose were anything ever to go wrong. Every Wendy's officer goes through a sixteen-hour program on food safety sanitation—everybody, including the top accountants and lawyers. We all take a test, including me. The way I see it, it's a responsibility thing. Some executive at headquarters isn't going to decide if a particular hamburger patty is fresh or if the temperature in the restaurant cooler is right, but those same execs are going to make decisions about buying tons of ground beef or deciding if we should offer a new type of sandwich that we don't have the right facilities to prepare. If they don't know the principles of sanitation inside out, how can they hope to help set the right direction?

Go for the longcut. Detours will take you to hell in a handbasket faster and surer than anything I know.

A lot of bosses I have seen are irresponsible in the ways they manage people. Bound and determined not to let their people do their jobs, they overmanage and direct employees in every little thing. They think that a person's job description is a rigid blueprint, and a boss's job is to take a bullhorn and shout marching orders into an employee's ear. Wendy's CEO Jim Near is just the greatest at giving people a wide enough berth to do their job and become stronger and more confident. Jim doesn't just live this while on the job, though. He has an absolutely great relationship with his wife and kids because he has a tremendous respect for them. And that respect comes out of Jim's sense of responsibility.

Responsibility means anticipating, and that's what Angel Grubb does to a "T" when she puts together my travel schedule so carefully. Responsibility means checking and double checking. That's sure true for our chief pilot Art Dunkle and his team. Before every flight, the crew go over the equipment and the flight plan as though their lives depend on it. They do—and no complaints from me, either. I fly over 120,000 miles a year, and, as much as I admire the guy, I'll take a pass on meeting St. Peter at the Pearly Gates because some airplane switch conked out.

Responsibility also means sometimes taking the heat on behalf of your company, your church, or your family. On my executive staff, Rosi Jinkens certainly knows the meaning of that because she and Marti Underwood help me write letters to customers. I get over three hundred letters a week and maybe a quarter of them deal with customer concerns. Believe me, Rosi will do her best to make things right for an unhappy customer until the matter is straightened out.

Why is dealing with customer concerns so important? "Can we really afford to lose one customer a day?" Rosi will ask. Can any business? What if a school loses one pupil, or a faith one loses one believer? If you're not there to answer the tough questions, they're sure to leave. And when one goes, you know what happens next.

Responsibility means doing the tough things, going out of your way to learn the right things, checking things backwards and forwards, and being big enough to take the heat— even if you aren't to blame. "Straight is the gate and narrow is the way." Right on!

GETTING GOVERNMENT TO LISTEN

One of the biggest responsibilities we Americans have is to get our government to listen. Almost all of us would agree that this isn't easy. The big reason—I think—is that we have forgotten how to talk to government. Government has encouraged the problem by talking to us like a bunch of bureaucrats half the time and treating us like children the other half. We tend to talk back to government the same way. How about trying some common sense instead?

South Carolina's Governor Carroll Campbell and I have become good friends. I'll say this—Carroll Campbell is a true statesman, one of the few around today. I say statesman because he puts the interests of his state before that of his career. He's a booster who really knows how to get something done, and I don't think that he would be playing golf with a guy like me unless he got something good out of it besides golf—because I'm sure not going to sharpen up anybody else's game.

I like to think of my relationship with Governor Campbell as my first true success in getting an idea picked up and put forward by a senior politician so that something major could happen. Over the years I've been practicing to try to do something like this, but now it may actually happen. And the cause is a good one: adoption benefits for all employees.

The problem is simple. In a company like Wendy's, we spend about $4,000 for an average birth through our maternity benefits. I'm all for that. Since 1990, traditional maternity benefits have cost us $6 million. In 1990 we added adoption coverage to our benefit plan. Eligible employees get paid leave and up to $4,000 in assistance when they adopt a child. The amount rises to $6,000 if the child has special needs. By special needs I mean that the child is older, is a part of a group of siblings who want to stay together, is from a minority culture, or is physically or mentally challenged.

For the average person, adoption can be a budget-boggling expense. There are legal costs and adoption agency fees, medical expenses and examinations, psychological evaluations and sometimes counseling, travel expenses, immunizations, and more.

Wendy's is not alone in offering adoption benefits. The consultants at Hewitt and Associates did a study in 1993 and found that eighteen percent of large companies with more than two thousand employees now offer benefits to employees looking to adopt. More should, and a growing number are, especially because the cost is really so small. Since we started offering adoption benefits in 1990, some nineteen Wendy's employees have adopted kids at a total cost to the company of $70,000. Compare that to the $6 million in maternity benefits we paid over the same period, and you'll see it's not a budget-breaker.

Also, adoption benefits are a family-friendly thing to do, and offering them attracts quality people to a company's work force.

The public sector is a real area of neglect for adoption benefits for employees. Presently, millions of people work for the public sector at some level or another—city, county, state, or federal. These people do not earn a huge hunk of money on a per-capita basis. A state worker in South Carolina, for example, has median annual wages of $21,000 a year. Taken against an average adoption cost nationwide of about $9,000, that's not much salary.

All this is very warm, loving, and decent, most people would say, but what's in it for the taxpayer? Enter Governor Campbell. He saw that there was plenty there for the taxpayer.

First, there are about 100,000 children available for adoption in the United States on any given day. Most are special-needs children. The cost for public support for unadopted children in the United States each year mounts up to an incredibly large figure.

Second, there are many good foster homes and some super foster parents, but the foster home idea has also come under the gun as some of them are in trouble. For instance, some have been run just to make money for the foster parents, and in a few others, neglect and abuse have taken place that have led to awful psychological or physical harm and even death.

Third, unadopted children are likelier to remain on public support rolls or to be tangled up in the criminal justice system. What would you expect from children who don't have the love, caring, and discipline of a home? Adoption benefits are a way of bringing children out of being wards of the state and back into the care of the private sector.

In January 1994, just before all those television reports that I went off to Lillehammer, Norway, to compete in the 120-meter ski jump, pairs figure skating, and the four-man bobsled (I won tin medals in every class), I went on my whistle-stop tour for adoption benefits. The first stop was Columbia, South Carolina, where I attended Governor Campbell's State-of-the-State address, in which he outlined his program for adoption.

In his speech, the Governor asked for a core benefit of $5,000 for a routine adoption and $10,000 in special needs cases. Added to that, new adoptive parents would get the regular six weeks of paid maternity leave and the child would have coverage under the state health insurance plan. South Carolina would be the first state in the nation to offer such a plan. He told me that there are many good reasons for supporting this program, and one of the best is that it "helps stabilize families, gets children out of the revolving door of foster care, and gives some kids a real crack at life."

Governor Campbell invited me to stay over at the governor's mansion. (The first time I was ever invited to stay in public housing I turned it down. Was that ever a mistake! President Ford had asked me to spend the night in Abraham Lincoln's White House bedroom, and I was too bashful to say yes. This time I wasn't gonna be so dumb.) You know where I got to sleep? In Scarlett O'Hara's bed, no less. Scarlett wasn't there; nobody was but me. (Lorraine was back home in Florida because some of the grandchildren were visiting.) Scarlett's bed had been donated as a prop from the David Selznick movie *Gone With the Wind*.

Then the governor invited me to talk to the National Governors' Association Winter Meetings held shortly thereafter in Washington D.C. Let me tell you, I may talk to millions of people on national T.V. via my ads, but it sure is a different story when you're on the podium in front of fifty governors at one time. But it's funny how speaking out for a good cause can give a person confidence. I made a bunch of little notes for the speech, but mostly I just talked from the heart. The one thing that I really stressed was the key reason we should be doing this: *It's fair.*

Governor Campbell suggested the other governors follow suit for their states in giving state employees adoption benefits. One day, hopefully, adoption benefits will reach federal employees, too. Think of the impact it would have on welfare benefits and other social programs, not to mention the longer-term impact on crime and on wasted lives.

I think we're going to be successful in seeing adoption benefits expanded state by state. Maybe you'll go out and campaign for it—I'd sure appreciate it—but the message here is broader than adoption. Perhaps another cause is closer to your heart. How do you mount a public campaign on a civic issue? Are there any overall lessons that came out of the way we tackled the adoption benefits program—lessons that can work in the village town hall as well as in the halls of Congress?

I can think of four:

- We went for the little clear picture. In the big picture, most people are for adoption, but there are also controversial adoption topics: open versus closed adoption, adoption by single parents, adoption by same-sex parents, adoption by older parents, and on and on. To push the cause of adoption one step further, we picked one small step and focused on employee benefits. It may sound very narrow, but this one step will probably lead to homes for thousands and thousands of children who otherwise wouldn't be adopted.

- We had pre-sold evidence. Adoption benefits were not a new, untried idea. State governments usually cannot afford to research their people to determine what benefits are important to them. Industry can, and far-sighted companies have learned that employees value adoption benefits. Remember, eighteen percent of companies have gone this way.

- We presented a pocket-book argument. There are many good things that could and should be done in the world, but we can't do them all. Many people try to persuade others on an issue by offering many good reasons—too many reasons. Instead, we gave just a few good *money-based* reasons why adoption benefits should be offered, and we also showed that the overall costs were low.

- Fourth, we teamed up with clout. If a smart, respected governor like Carroll Campbell hadn't raised his saber and led the charge, nobody would have let this old boy thump his wares on Pennsylvania Avenue. The Guv knows this, and he isn't boasting when he describes how things are helped to happen in the world of government. "It's like an auction," he says. "When a governor gets up and sells something, you get a better price."

MAKING A SPECTACLE OF SUCCESS

Being a media celebrity can be a weird life from time to time; sometimes making a spectacle of yourself is the price of success. For nearly seventy years, Macy's has sponsored the annual Thanksgiving Day Parade down Broadway to 34th Street, and I got invited to be part of the 1993 parade. This was some bash, I'll tell you. Stevie Wonder was there; Dr. Joyce Brothers coasted along on the Mother Duck float; stars from the 1969 New York Mets showed up. The Spider-Man Balloon looked awesome.

Me, I was sort of Santa's advance man because Santa's float was not far behind the one I was on. On the float with me were castmembers of the musical *Annie Warbucks*: Harve Presnell who plays Daddy Warbucks, Kathryn Zaremba who plays Annie—and I can't forget Cindy Lou who plays the dog

Sandy. After Harve and Kathryn finished one of the numbers from the show, I flipped a switch and all the lights on a huge Christmas tree sitting on the float turned on.

It was fun, but it was cold, too. When we turned from Central Park West onto Broadway, I felt like I was being sucked into a wind tunnel—even with two pairs of long johns, a thermal top, and flannel shirts. I guess it's okay to roll down Broadway in the company of huge hot-air balloons and to hear that spongy thump as they bounce off lampposts and bang into skyscrapers along the concrete canyon. After all, plenty of people see you on T.V.. But I did it for only one real reason, and that was to call attention to the adoption message. Comments came in from all over the country that said we had lit a few candles for the sake of adoption. We may even have given a couple of kids homes for Christmas.

If you're smart, you'll always get a cute kid to upstage you. That way you can't lose—W. C. Fields taught the world that. Annie did it for Daddy Warbucks and me in the parade, and a little girl named Brittany did it for Paul Azinger in the 1993 Wendy's Three-Tour Challenge golf event played on Hilton Head Island's Colleton River Plantation Course in South Carolina, which was broadcast on Christmas Day. The Three-Tour Challenge pits three mixed threesomes from the Senior, Men's, and Women's PGA Tours against each other. The women won the first year, and Ray Floyd of the Seniors shot a course record 62 to win the second year's tourney. A lot of adoption messages were shown during the telecast in 1993, and we got more than 3,000 calls on the adoption hotline.[1]

One reason so many folks called in, I think, was something Paul Azinger did on the eighteenth hole. I couldn't have scripted it any better! Paul, a great golfer, was having a decent day but not an outstanding one as he played against Chi Chi Rodriguez and Patty Sheehan. Just as Paul was walking onto

---

1. For anyone interested in adoption of special needs children, the adoption hotline number is 1-800-TO-ADOPT (862-3678).

the green, a baby started to cry in the gallery. Paul looked up and said, "Awww, darlin', that's exactly how I feel."

The audience chuckled. Paul marked his ball. And the baby went on speaking her mind in a way only babies can. Well, Paul decided, what the heck? He found the little girl among the crowd—a child named Brittany, about eighteen months old—and carried her toward the green. The spectators first started laughing, then began to cheer.

Paul lined her up with his putter and helped her putt. They missed the hole by about a foot. Brittany was really getting into it by then; she walked up to the ball, picked it up and looked around at the assembled masses. Folks began shouting, "Put the ball in the hole!" She plunked the ball in the hole, then took it out again and proudly brought it back to Mommy.

The cheers were deafening! And none of this was rehearsed. The big thing was that Paul momentarily put his own game on the sideline to shine the spotlight on kids, because that's what this tourney was about. Paul is fighting a battle with lymphoma cancer right now, and he should know that there are a lot of people rooting on the side of this big-hearted guy.

Well done, Paul Azinger!

When the NAACP decided to confer their first ever Humanitarian Award on me in the spring of 1994 I was flabbergasted, not really knowing what I had done to deserve such an honor. But I accepted it, mostly because the media attention would help drive home the point that adoption is a really important cause to Americans of all backgrounds. When NAACP Chairman Dr. William Gibson handed me that award in New York City, we both knew down deep, I felt, that we were honoring an idea and a goal a heck of a lot bigger than Dave Thomas.

There's a lesson here. I think that successful people—modestly successful or big-time successful—are obliged to use their success to draw attention to worthwhile causes. I've believed this for more than twenty years.

It doesn't have to be national television, and it doesn't have to happen in the middle of Manhattan on Thanksgiving Day: it can be in a small, rural farm community where a championship Little League team can bring out supporters to back buying the local clinic a new kidney dialysis machine. In business, it can happen by having the top executives play in a company's softball tourney to raise money for that company's tutoring program. Even someone who wins a big lottery prize and turns over a hunk of that money to charity is making a statement.

Something that almost always happens when success is used this way is that it helps out your own business and personal goals. That's not *why* you do it, but it somehow seems to just happen. It happened on national television during the Macy's parade, when NBC's Willard Scott said, "There's Mr. Wendy there—I'm going to fix him a hamburger." Remember, Willard, adoption first. Willard—what a guy!

COURAGE

We tend to make courage too dramatic. Courage is often doing something simple, unpleasant, or boring again and again until we get it down pat. People who are physically challenged and who have the determination to get around their handicaps or boundaries are great examples because their courage makes them test their limits every day in a way that the rest of us write off as small-time.

Maybe the most courageous people of all are those who know they face death or a serious handicap, yet who climb above themselves and their own hurt to put others first.

If you think about courage, I say that you should start by thinking about the little things—the little first steps especially. My daughter Lori has always been the baby of the family. Everybody thinks that's a swell place in line to have, but it isn't always. Sure, people may spoil you some of the time, but you also get advice until it comes out of your ears—from your parents, and from your brothers and sisters, too. Just recently, Lori and her husband John headed out to Arizona, where they plan to get a franchise for a Wendy's restaurant. They did a pretty careful job of studying and researching the idea up front, and I want to congratulate Lori. She may succeed; she may fail. But I want to congratulate her anyway, because she and her husband are taking a risk, and they're on their own. Often parents and older kids won't let go of their baby. And it's easy for the baby to lean back—but Lori isn't our baby anymore.

JACK IN THE CATBIRD SEAT

Jack Hutchings is a rich guy. He's one of the most successful suppliers to the auto industry in Detroit, and his house may be the biggest in Ft. Lauderdale. He likes to sit high on the flying bridge of Lady Colombo, his boat, as she cruises down the Intracoastal Waterway by upper-crust condominiums and luxury homes. The Intracoastal, which links Miami and Ft. Lauderdale and spans much of Florida's Atlantic Coast, was built as an inland haven for America's naval fleet around the time of World War II. Today it's just like Interstate 75—only with hot-rodding and cigarette boats shooting down the lanes.

We come up on Turnberry Isle—one classy place and home to plenty of the rich and the famous—and I say to Jack: "All those lights on over there and all that commotion . . . must be plenty of parties tonight." He smiles and nods his head.

The lights of the Intracoastal, probably the highest class back alley in all of America, glisten tonight. The steak houses and the lobster joints, Turnberry Isle and Port Everglades—I can see it all, but Jack can't see anything.

Jack is blind—a victim of retinitis pigmentosa. It's hard enough to say that disease, let alone spell it. Jack's a great friend and a heck of a success story. He even won the Horatio Alger Award because he climbed so high out of such a miserable start.

Jack told me that his parents were heavy drinkers who used to stash him in the family jalopy in Jack's hometown of Pontiac, Michigan, while they went to a bar to booze it up. In the end, they dumped him. Get lost, buddy. By age sixteen, Jack was legally blind and on his own. By age thirty, the lights in his eyes were out forever.

But Jack was and is a special person.

First of all, he's a singer. And a rocker. He crooned with a group known as the High Tones. Maybe he could have been the next Ray Charles or Stevie Wonder. Jack even went to

Interlochen in northern Michigan during the summers, which has a music camp that is *the* address for talented young musicians and singers. He won a scholarship to the New York Conservatory of Music, but he never went there. In fact, he never went to college at all.

Jack made his first career as a soda jerk in a Kresge five-and-dime. Career goal: Mister Straw. He yearned to be the soda-fountain manager at Pontiac's newest Kresge store back in the sixties, but since he wasn't twenty-one yet, Kresge didn't want him for the job. So he went to work for a little company that made tubing. He learned tubing backwards and forwards, upwards and downwards.

Then he decided to go out on his own and began to bend tubing in the garage next to his home. Still depending on his own sight—sight that was growing dimmer by the day—he bent tubes under a forty-watt bulb. At first it was tough to get the business to work, so tough that Sears repossessed his storm windows when he couldn't make the payments. Jack was used to disappointments like that. When he walked through the door of the first house he had bought, his foot went through the floor.

Despite it all, Jack stuck with it. Air conditioning was coming on big for automakers of the sixties and seventies, and Jack Hutchings had the courage to make the most of that trend. A car can't have air conditioning unless it had coiled pipe. He knew that air conditioning would one day be an almost standard feature on American cars, so that became Jack's focus: shaping and delivering coiled pipe to biggies like General Motors. He made a mint.

Jack travels a lot these days on one of his company's two jets to keep track of all his operations. When he goes to a hotel, the front desk often wants to give him a suite. He says, "Don't give me a suite. Give me a small room. I don't need luxury. I need to find my way around." He's having a boat custom-built right now—one where he can be dead sure of where the head is (sailor talk for a bathroom). Why a boat? Why would a blind guy want a boat to cruise up and down the Intracoastal if he can't see the lights or the water or the buildings? He loves to feel that salty breeze lick his face and to hear the waves and wakes lapping against the hull. That's what the catbird seat means to him.

Jack knows cars inside out. How are American cars today compared with the Japanese? Better, Jack says, except in the paint. Do you know he can actually feel the finish of the paint and its quality?

Jack's firm has sixteen plants throughout North America today. How does he do it? He can't look at profit-and-loss statements or computer screens. He can't even look at people. "I know what's right by talking," Jack says. I've been with him, and I swear it's true. So does Jack. He can tell you about what's right and wrong with a plant by the way the machinery runs or how the footsteps in it sound. He listens for the caution or the hesitations in people's voices. Since he has plants in Mexico now, he's starting Spanish lessons. He was thinking about Latin America long before NAFTA came down the pike.

When General Motors sent twenty people worldwide to meet Jack in a reception room not long ago, he stretched his hand out to meet each one. He did it—hand forward, hand back. He did it in the right place and at the right time because he listened to the height the voices were coming from and the rustle of an arm moving in a suit. It takes courage to learn those kinds of moves and to be willing to try them out.

And Jack still water skis! We're about the same age, and me—I worry about slipping in the shower. Do you know what Jack's explanation is for what he does? "What's the alternative?" What *is* the alternative? Groping around for a cane or an excuse?

Well done, Jack Hutchings!

The blind leading the sighted. Not a bad idea sometimes. You know what's the capper? When I'm with other managers and we talk about executives who really have the courage to forge a fresh, clean vision for their businesses, the first manager I always think of is Jack Hutchings.

STANDS ARE GOOD. STEPS ARE BETTER.

You don't have to be standing on the front lines of a bat-
tlefield pulling the pin out of a grenade with your teeth to be
courageous. Sometimes courage is just taking a stand and
then backing it up with quiet actions. As a dues-paying member of the Screen Actor's Guild, let me give you some views on
what I think being responsible and courageous in the entertainment industry means today.

"Hooray for Hollywood!" some say. Well, not always.
Hollywood used to be great at spelling out our dreams or giving us a lift with its jokes and its gags. It's too bad that there's
such little good-natured humor left on television or in films.
The movies I like are almost all funny ones. I'm a big Bob Hope
fan. Who could forget Bob Hope and Jimmy Cagney in their
vaudeville dance duet in *The Seven Little Foys*? Or, Bob Hope,
Bing Crosby, and Dorothy Lamour in *The Road to Rio*? As for
today's actors, I liked Michael Keaton heaps in *Mr. Mom*, but
not in *Batman*. Why did they have to do Batman in the bedroom, anyway? Here was a good, old-fashioned role model—
the kind that kids still need today—turned into a high-flying
playboy. Humor is important, but I don't find that much of
what is happening in the entertainment world today is much
of a laughing matter.

Wendy's commercials are on television a lot, and that
means I am on television a lot. Okay by me, provided I'm hanging out in the right place. That's harder than you may think.
"What do you mean by that?" people will ask me. "You guys at
Wendy's pay for the ad, don't you? Don't you control where the
ad gets put?" The truth is, television schedules change. A football game goes into sudden death overtime or the network
runs a news special, and a local station may pull its planned
program and shove something else in instead. Sometimes the
VCR at the station will break down or the engineer on duty
may forget to punch the right button. Then they give an adver-

tiser a "make-good" to make up for the ad that never aired—
then "watch out!", because make-goods can be bad news. You
may have thought you were buying time in "The Adventures of
Goldilocks" only to have your ad end up in the middle of
"Chainsaw Massacre in Blood Valley."

In the fall of 1993 some people wrote Wendy's letters
about our advertising on national television programs. Unlike
many companies, we wrote everybody back and called many of
the people who had written in. They were shocked that we took
the time, and some were impressed with, or at least understanding of, what we had to say.

Some of the movies we sponsored that the write-in campaign attacked were the slick, raw, and salty films that seem to
be what Hollywood churns out and which also win so many
Academy Awards year after year. Others, critics say, are works
of art—like *The Color Purple*—and deciding whether to spon-
sor them is a real judgment call. We now have a list of shows
on which we won't advertise—including plenty of talk shows
and T.V. tabloids. We even have to watch out which cartoons
you buy. A Wendy's ad can show up in *Tom & Jerry*, but I can
guarantee you it won't be rubbing shoulders with Beavis and
Butthead.

We do have controls set up. They work better nationally
than they do locally just because there are so many stations
broadcasting across the country these days, but we're getting
better locally, too. Still, controls are really not the answer.
You're not going to get some pitch from me now on First
Amendment rights—although I believe in them. The problem
is that not enough entertainment companies out there are
funding the making of family entertainment programs. If we
all feel this way, the answer is to do something positive.

Why are we concerned? Because the same shows that deliver strong ratings for excessive violence, sex, and profanity for
adults deliver an identical audience for teenagers and children.

In a recent *Gallup Poll* Americans said there is too much

violence on T.V., that it is related to the country's crime rate, and the network warning labels do not go far enough in alerting parents to objectionable programming content. Parents are saying they want T.V. more closely regulated.

Many viewers are also stating they will *not* buy products advertised in offending shows. In a separate survey, almost two-thirds of adults found television sex and violence offensive. Importantly, nearly half of this group stated they would no longer consider purchasing products advertised in these programs. Therefore, it appears that advertising in a T.V. show with offensive program content may harm a consumer's perception of a company's image or reputation.

In November 1993, Charlie Rath and I went to New York to the headquarters of ABC/Capitol Cities on Central Park West. We have had a bunch of talks with heads of the networks in recent months, and the topic is always the same: Wendy's wants to encourage the development of more family-oriented and wholesome programming at advertising rates that will attract advertisers. We said we are afraid that Wendy's is going to be shut out of buying advertising time during prime-time network shows because the sex, violence, and foul language on so many prime-time programs doesn't match up with our image as a family restaurant.

We put a number of ideas on the table. We said that it's counterproductive for the networks and big advertisers to be on opposite sides of this debate: People want clean, sensible programming for their families. Families buy the lion's share of the products, and the big companies who make and sell those products want to present them on network television. The networks, we said, should consider carving out dedicated time slots each evening—maybe the first hour or so of prime time—to be used *only* for family programming, and see if that kind of plan would get backing from major sponsors. My bet is that sponsors of all sorts would rush for that time slot. We also said that we would write a position paper on what we advertisers should do if we are to make advances on the programming content issue.[1]

Our paper—we call it "the white paper"—states that headway in improving television programming will be made only if advertisers take the initiative. In turn, that will only happen when advertisers appreciate that wholesome programming is effective in reaching key audiences. When this truth sinks in, advertisers are sure to sound off against objectionable programs and encourage the success and increasing number of good family programs.

I really expect us to make some progress this way. There's a big lesson here, and it's not about advertising or even about values. It's about standing up for what you believe in. Instead of spending time and energy hollering about what's wrong, (1) figure out what should be right instead, (2) give people the incentive to do the right thing, and (3) start small enough so that you can give the program strong legs and a real base of support. That's what practical courage is all about.

LORRAINE—STUDY IN SPUNK

Women have more guts than men. I really believe that. My wife Lorraine is the gutsiest woman I've ever met since my grandma Minnie Sinclair. Today Lorraine is president of the Royal Dames—an organization that raises money in the battle against cancer—and she's also an active campaigner for the Children's Home Society in Florida, doing some fundraising on behalf of this outfit's wonderful professional staff like Pat Sizer. Her big project now is the building and opening of the I. Lorraine Thomas Emergency Home and Family Support Center—a home for children in family crisis. Lorraine's always been tough and determined, but she was always shy about

---

1. The white paper has since been written and if you would like a copy, please write to Consumer Relations at Wendy's International, Inc., P.O. Box 256, Dublin, OH 43017.

speaking in public. Fundraising has changed all that over the past five years, and today she can gavel a meeting and knock out a talk with the best of them. After raising a pack of kids, it has been a whole new career. And has she excelled at it!

I don't know what exactly made me fall for Lorraine, but I sure fell, and I've never regretted it. She has spunk. Lorraine even has an aunt who was a preacher in the tiny town of Pipe Creek, Ohio, just outside of Bellaire, who continues to send us tracts in the mail to this day. My wife grew up going to prayer meetings at her home-town fundamentalist church every Wednesday evening and twice on Sundays.

Lorraine's grandfather ran a grocery store—an old-fashioned community store—and carried the local miners on account during lean times. Lorraine's parents were divorced when she was just a baby, and her mother worked at the Marx Toy Factory in Glendale, West Virginia—a place where they used to make doll houses and cutout toy metal buildings. Lorraine says that she really didn't mind being in a split home all that much as a kid because there was always plenty of family around. But she does remember one difference: Her sister was raised by her grandmother and aunt and brought up more conservatively than Lorraine, who lived with her mother. At the very same time of year, Lorraine's sister would be wearing long skirts and knee socks while Lorraine got away with shorts.

Being home alone a lot, Lorraine got to be pretty handy with a screwdriver at fixing things. She's still better at it than I am. She learned to be self-reliant when she was very young. One of her earliest memories was standing on a wooden chair stirring up cottage-fried potatoes with a wooden spoon over a sizzling cast-iron skillet.

Lorraine knows how to handle herself when things get tough. I remember when our daughter Wendy was eleven years old—I can't believe it was already twenty years ago—and she was out riding her bike along with a girlfriend. They turned a corner and hit gravel. Wendy lunged forward and the handlebars of the bike badly bruised her right kidney. The doctors had to repair the major artery going through her kidney. It was then that we learned that Wendy's other kidney was already not working. It was touch and go. We didn't know a surgeon, and I was on business out of the country, so I took the first flight back.

I'll be honest: I'm not so good in hospitals. I was scared, but we were lucky that the doctors were great, and Wendy pulled through just fine.

Lorraine is a rock when things like that happen—like the time Kenny put his hand through a plate glass window. She'll keep the spirits up of the person who is sick or injured and will talk with the doctors and reassure everybody in the family. Me? I'm usually coasting toward the exit sign. Lorraine gets pretty exasperated with me. At times like that, she'll even turn to a perfect stranger and say, "I've got a deal for you. How would you feel about adopting Dave?"

Lorraine's a super organizer—never a better arranger than when she put together "The Great Family Photograph." When our youngest daughter got married in the spring of 1993, we had one of those few chances when the family would be all together. We have thirteen grandchildren now, and when we show people a picture of the whole family together, it's pretty hard to keep everybody straight. So Lorraine cooked up this idea of putting each of the "subfamilies" in a different color T-shirt. Pam and her brood wore lavender, Kenny's bunch wore pink. There was also a dark blue team, a turquoise team, and a rose team.

At first, I thought this whole idea was for the birds; so did my son Kenny. But Lorraine stuck with it and had a heck of a way of doing it. First she said, "This is all I'm asking." Then she said, "This is all I'm asking . . . and now I'm telling, not asking." The picture was taken and it hangs in the most important spot in our family room. I've decided it's the favorite photo I've ever had. (But do me a favor: Don't tell Lorraine any of this.)

CANCER COURAGEOUS

Cancer has long been a big target for whatever giving my friends have done for the community. Pessimists have always said that cancer was an unbeatable disease, but my friends are a feisty lot. "What a bunch of baloney that you can't beat cancer," people I respected would say. I go along with that.

When it comes to success and cancer, not a lot of people would put those two words together. After all, cancer is such an awful thing that we just don't want to talk about it. In fact, as far as health goes, cancer is the dirtiest six-letter word in the book.

Well, let's talk dirty. If you're going to be successful in life, I think that you have to talk about things that may scare you or make you queasy. Cancer is one of those things.

Dr. Arthur James is one of the finest cancer doctors around. He decided that he was going to specialize in cancer way back in 1939. He actually started his cancer practice in Columbus in 1948 and stopped caring for patients in 1990. Not long ago I asked Dr. James to describe to me two of his most successful cancer patients. I didn't make it easy; I asked him for two kinds of patients—one who had cancer, really bad cancer, and who survived and had a great attitude. Then I asked him to talk about someone who didn't make it but still had a great attitude and made the people around him or her feel good until life was over.

Dr. James wrestled with this for a few days, because he has gotten to know some very special people over the years. It was hard for him to single particular people out, but two finally stood out as I explained what we were trying to do with this book. The first is Lois Gruenbaum, and the second is Denny Clark.

Lois Gruenbaum grew up in Cleveland and went to work in a hospital kitchen when she was just fifteen. During World War II she became a nurse's aide and worked in an army hospital for six months. The hospital made an impression on her. She would go home after her shift and say to herself, "Hey, things can be bad, but there's always somebody who can be worse off. All you need to do is find out what you can't do and then go ahead and do what you can do."

Great lesson—and Lois learned it not long before she needed to put it to use. In 1955 she got what Dr. James called "a very nasty tumor of the pelvis." Operation followed operation, but it still came back. The next time the cutting was going to be deep and hard: It was going to change her life radically forever. Dr. James told Lois that the only choice was to take one leg off completely and one-half of the pelvic bone on that side of her body. Lois didn't flinch. She told the doctor to do it.

On November 21, 1955, Lois had the surgery and came home from the hospital only two days before Christmas. She returned home to her family: a husband, a seven-year-old, a four-year-old, and two-year-old twins. The surgery was so deep she couldn't really wear an artificial limb; she was going to have to live her life on crutches.

Thank God that the two-year-olds were potty-trained. If you ask her how she was able to cope, she'll tell you that it was simple: She had no choice. She says that she cut a deal with the Lord and the Lord apparently listened. "I promised the Lord," Lois says, "that if He let me live to raise my children, I would not vegetate. I would be a contributing person." Her optimism spread faster and deeper than her cancer. Her four kids grew up with a belief that Lois puts this way: "Mom got along for all those years without a leg. I guess I can get over this hurdle."

Lois can tell stories about life on one leg, some of which will tear you up laughing and some that will bring a tear to your eye. Not long after the operation, her six-year-old came into the kitchen while mom was fixing dinner and asked, "Mommy, when are you going to get another leg?" All the other mommies had two legs, he figured. Lois was really smart (maybe a better word is wise). She asked her son, "Danny, why do I need another leg? Don't we go swimming? Don't we go on picnics? Don't we go on trips?" What an answer! Her little guy saw the light.

But the way that guys looked at her may have been the funniest thing of all. One little fellow asked her how she could swim with just one leg, and her answer was "Have you ever seen a mermaid with two feet?" One day a local Columbus VIP noted for taking a nip or two flirted with her while he was a bit snookered and said, "Didn't matter at all that they took the one leg off, the one that you have left is pretty good lookin'!"

It's almost forty years later, and Lois will be the first to tell you that she's had a great deal of fun in her life. Wonderful husband. Great kids. Would she have had any of this if she had given up? If she didn't believe in herself, could she have had the courage to go to cancer wards to encourage other patients, to be a city-hall reporter for a local radio station, and to keep her bags "partially packed" so that she is always ready to take off with her husband on the next business trip if she didn't believe in herself? This lady is "attitude" in capital letters.

Denny Clark's life took a different course, but Denny and Lois were cut out of the same cloth. Fighters both. Denny was in the insurance business. My wife Lorraine knows his widow Jean, who is a nurse, and Wendy went to camp with one of the Clark kids.

Denny had his first bout with cancer when he was thirty-one. He had five cancer operations in a row—two before coming to Dr. James—followed by radiation and chemotherapy, too. Then things looked good. It seemed to Denny and Dr. James that Denny had licked the cancer, that the remission had taken.

When he was about fifty, cancer came calling on Denny for a second visit—this time with a vengeance. It turned out that his cancer was the sort that came on strong, then laid dormant, and after years would return full bore. Denny had a leg and half his hip amputated, but even that didn't stop the tumors. Between 1982 and 1986 he had major surgery each year.

I never met Denny personally, but who can doubt he was

a real fighter? The people who knew him glow when they talk about him. His wife, who's German, says part of the reason was that Denny was Irish. She and her son Bill also think that Denny's dogged belief in PMA, Positive Mental Attitude, had plenty to do with Denny's ability to climb out of the valleys in his life. He built a great insurance practice, became president of first the local and then the state Association of Life Underwriters, bought an office condominium, and helped his three sons build their practices.

Denny could laugh, too. When children asked, after the amputation, what happened to his leg, he said, "The alligator ate it." When Denny got a prosthetic replacement, he called his new member "Charo"—after that firey Latin bombshell who was such a big hit on the talk shows of the time. Denny and Jean would still dance at receptions, even though Jean remembers that she would do most of the moving. He would still ride over the course in the golf cart, and he could even take some swings if Jean helped prop him up a little. Later he learned to play without assistance.

Denny loved his work and thought that the insurance profession was the greatest business in the world. When the second cancer came, he didn't sit back waiting for somebody to fluff his pillow. Between bad bouts of the illness or major operations, he'd go into the office and meet clients. Toward the end, he would meet with clients in the kitchen or living room of his home. He just wouldn't let go of his career or the profession that he was so proud of.

"I had him dead at least a half dozen times," Jean says, but he hung on. Maybe another drive that kept Denny going was that both of his parents died young from cancer. He wanted to provide. He wanted to guide. He was a builder. And he was a worker.

No doubt, one thing that helped keep Denny going so long was the love and support of his family as well as great doctors like Dr. James. But Denny also had drive and determination. He stayed busy in the world instead of drifting down into the misery of his illness. Denny Clark didn't lose his fight with cancer; he won it big time because he did so much more than anyone around him thought it was humanly possible to do, and because he was, is, and will be such an inspiration to others.

What makes people like Lois Gruenbaum and Denny Clark tick, I think, is that they are able to stay in touch with the "well" life going on around them. They overcome everything because they want to help other people meet their challenges and achieve their goals. Among other things, courage means stepping out and putting yourself second—even when the pain and misery inside you wants you to put you first.

Dr. Michael Lerner is an expert on alternative cancer therapies who runs group training sessions with cancer patients and helps them live longer, better lives by teaching them how to relax and cut down stress. Once these folks realize the new skills they are learning, Dr. Lerner points out, "People will sit around the room together and say, 'It's crazy that I had to get cancer to learn this stuff.'" [2]

You can learn courage anytime, too. I'm sure that Lois and Denny learned courage long before they got cancer and their courage was tested. Anytime . . . why not right now?

---

2. Bill Moyers, *Healing and the Mind* (New York: Doubleday, 1993), p. 334.

GENEROSITY

A person who has modest means and won't share may be considered stingy. But rich people can give 'til they're purple and still not be truly generous. One of the things I'm proudest about in the Wendy's family is that so many franchisees make significant donations to the community—and they contribute leadership as well as dollars. If you're not giving of yourself as much as you're giving of your wallet, are you really generous down deep? We should work hard to make the Virtuous Circle of Generosity the number-one epidemic in the United States— giving of wealth, giving of self. Unstoppable and unending.

My old friend the late Kenny King—gee, do I still miss him—was a generous guy who had a real knack for how he gave. He really took pleasure in it, was modest about it, and he was often anonymous, but he really tried to learn what giving was all about. Even when he gave people moral support, he would say, "I'm really getting a lot more out of this than you are." I can't tell you how many times he said that to me. Later, when I tried to do for others what Kenny had done for me, I learned what he meant. When you give people help and understanding, you truly learn what people are like. And those who understand others better are certainly the most likely to succeed. The giving and the getting become all mixed up—which I think is great.

THE PROUD BEGGAR

In February of 1991 I had to take a trip to Memphis. It wasn't a trip I wanted to make, and it all happened suddenly. I had to say goodbye to a friend.

There's a church in Memphis I'll never forget. You don't forget places where you say goodbye to your best friends. It's plenty bigger than Calvary Church in Kalamazoo where I had my first memories of going to church. In fact, it's a cathedral—the Cathedral of the Immaculate Conception. It looks sort of Spanish on the outside. All I can say for sure is that, on the inside, it's mighty fancy and super big. It's supposed to be one of the biggest churches in all of the southern United States, and that I have to believe.

But although it may be big, on that day in 1991 when I was there, there was no seat to be had and people were lined up on the steps out front. A lot of other people—not just me—had lost a friend.

"O Danny Boy, the pipes, the pipes are calling.
From glen to glen and down the mountainside.
The summer's gone—all the roses falling.
It's you. It's you must go, and I must bide."

A song you'd expect to hear in an Irish pub, not in a cathedral. You wouldn't expect it to be sung by a Metropolitan Opera soprano like Marguerite Piazza either. Maybe you'd think that it was honoring an Irish cardinal, but who would expect that it would be sung in memory of a Lebanese entertainer? We were all standing as the song filled the church. The children's choir and a full symphony chimed in from up in the choir loft.

People's eyes were tearing before the music started, but when folks heard the first notes of that song—Danny Thomas's theme song for decades—everybody choked up. Most of us couldn't hold back any longer. A little girl and an older couple were crying, and I don't know what sounds seemed bigger to my ears—the crying or the music. Joe Karam—a first-class gentleman and the person who introduced me to Danny—was standing by my side. Joe was one of Danny's closest friends, and I remember, as I looked at Joe, how much he resembled Danny—the nose, the eyes, the other features of his face.

Pall bearers brought Danny's casket down the main aisle, under the huge gold dome. It was eerie, because the cathedral is kind of coral on the inside, and the light was nearly pink as it poured through the big stained glass windows. It was eerie, too, knowing that Danny's body was inside that coffin, because I had clowned around with him on the phone just a few days earlier. It made me think real hard about who we had lost.

Danny was a great friend. He was not a relative, even though we have the same last name. No doubt about it, he was one heck of an entertainer and showman. But, most of all, he was a great, great humanitarian.

An obsession drove Danny Thomas—the St. Jude's Children's Hospital in Memphis. He'd do anything for that hospital. Danny was such a great success in life. No man or woman I know ever got over every inch of that false pride that we are all born with more than Danny did. He called himself "The Proud Beggar," and he called other people who helped him raise money for St. Jude the same thing.

If Danny Thomas hadn't forgotten a promise, St. Jude would never have been built. Yes, forgotten, and let me tell you why. Back in 1943 Danny was still playing five-dollar-a-week gigs. His wife was pregnant with their first—Marlo. (Marlo, we all know, went on to be a famous actress herself and is today married to the talk-show host Phil Donahue.) The couple needed money to raise a family. Danny's wife's uncle was a butcher and offered Danny a job cutting meat, but he wanted to stay in show business. Danny stopped at a church and, in his Catholic tradition, prayed to St. Jude for direction. He asked to be shown which path to take: should he be a comedian or a butcher? Not much later, Danny got booked at Chez Paris in Chicago. He made it big time. The booking lasted for five years, and he went straight from no-name nightclubs to network T.V.

Meanwhile, Danny had forgotten all about his promise until well into his stint at Chez Paris. Forgetting to make good on a promise was about the worst thing a person could do, in Danny's book. When he finally remembered his promise, he went to see Cardinal Stritch in Chicago—an old buddy of his—and asked the cardinal what he should do. The cardinal told him that we already had enough churches and enough statues. The cardinal, whose first parish was in Memphis, gave him the idea of starting a children's hospital there. That's what Danny did; he built the best children's hospital in all of the world.

Why is the place named after St. Jude? St. Jude is the saint in charge of impossible acts. Danny felt that "no child should die in the dawn of life," so he declared a personal war against the killer diseases that strike children. He started funding the hospital in Memphis in 1957. Great names in medicine like Dr. Donald Pinkle and Dr. Joseph Simone led the research at St. Jude.

Plenty of impossible things were made possible because Danny stuck with his mission like a bulldog. In 1962 only 4% of the victims of acute lymphocytic leukemia survived the disease; in 1991 73% survived. Only 7% of patients with non-Hodgkin lymphoma recovered in 1962; about thirty years later, 80% did. The list goes on and on. When people talk about the "impossible" in medicine, just think of St. Jude and what was done there.

In 1991, Danny Thomas was doing fundraising for St. Jude—he always did fundraising for the hospital before taking on jobs that would put money in his own pocket. He was also promoting his own book, the proceeds from which went to the hospital. One night he got home late. He was worn out. At 2:30 in the morning a massive heart attack killed him.

The pink glow inside the Memphis cathedral on that special day in 1991 is a memory that I will never lose, just as I won't forget where Danny is laid to rest. He's not buried in some grassy cemetery; he is buried in a mausoleum inside the hospital. All around the mausoleum you see Danny's favorite sayings—sayings like: "Blessed is the man who knows why he was born," and "He who denies his heritage has no heritage."

Danny gave himself. He taught others to give themselves, too, and to forget their selfish side. I remember him saying to one donor who had put down a large hunk of change for St. Jude, "The deepest thank-you I can give is to pray that you and yours will never need the help of St. Jude's Hospital." Isn't that the truth about any charity that helps people out of disasters? It's a thank-you worth remembering when you're raising money for charities, so don't be afraid to use something like it. And it's an idea sure worth remembering when you're giving money to charities too.

Well done, Danny boy!

Danny is somebody worth remembering anytime the temptation comes up for "me" to take over "we." Everything that made Danny Danny has simple roots:

- Keep your word. Danny kept his word to God.

- Let a good cause that's bigger than you are take over your life. What is your St. Jude? There ought to be one; think about it and fund it.

- Don't get scared by the word *impossible*. In fact, get together the best talents you can find to tackle the impossible.

- Do it through people. Danny got well people and well-healed people to work on behalf of unfortunate people. That's the way it should be, isn't it?

- And, when you're passing the hat for a good cause, you can be proud to be a beggar. Real proud.

My Yacht For Your Golf Course

I once had a really big yacht—a ninety-one-foot Broward power boat, but I got tired of it: it was too hard to park! So I traded it for a golf course—The Woodlands Golf Course in Columbia, South Carolina. Then I gave Ken McCarthy, who had been captain of the boat, two minutes to decide if he wanted to try his hand at running a golf course. He said yes. I not only knew that he would, I also knew he'd do a good job at it. Ken has.

Today, I still have a boat, although it's only about half as long (easier to park, too). Brad Treliving is my captain but I love to sail it myself. Boating has been a big hobby of mine for a long time; ever since we were able to afford it, we've had power boats and then cruisers. That started back in Ohio, first on Buckeye Lake and then on the Ohio River. My son Kenny— not to be confused with Ken McCarthy—got more of a kick out of it than my daughters, I think. This was before we had any professional crew members, of course. I went down to the army surplus store and got some sergeant stripes, lieutenant bars, and general stars (guess who got to wear the general stars?). All the members of the family crew got to swab decks and do other chores. Friends would get on me, saying that I got my branches of service screwed up with the insignia. I guess I thought of myself as an amphibious army.

So we worked our way up through the boat classes and finally got the yacht. That's when the golf-course proposition came up. During my life, I'd played on enough golf courses— not with any great distinction mind you—and I'd hacked up my share of divots. This particular golf course had its problems: It had lost some seventy members in the six months before I got the deed to it. The yacht/golf-course swap started out as a business deal, but it also has a lesson in it about helping out the community. Even that help, though, had its roots in how we straightened out the business of the golf course. There's a clue in that I wouldn't pass up.

I figured that we really only needed to do three things to put this club back on its feet. First, we had to straighten out the course. Second, we needed to expand the grill room with a nice simple menu, offering good food at fair prices and *no gourmet*. Third, we had to give the community a reason to be interested in the golf course. Easy enough. We did the first two things in less than a year, and then we organized a golf tournament as a charity fundraiser. In three years, all the tournament spots filled up, and now the golf course is doing just fine, thank you. It's been a great opportunity to use the blessings God has given me to have some fun and to raise some money for a good cause.

A friend of mine in Toronto, Canada, named Ron Joyce, did the same thing a few years back. Ron is CEO of a chain of donut shops called Tim Hortons. Back in 1974, there were only forty shops; now there are more than eight hundred scattered across Canada. In '74, Ron's partner Tim Horton was killed in a tragic car accident. Ron felt a strong need to remember Tim's passing in a way that would have made Tim proud, so he built a camp for financially disadvantaged children outside of Toronto. This was a big project for what was still just a growing company back then, but the camp got built—mortgaged to the hilt—and only because of scads of volunteer time on weekends.

My point is that Ron didn't wait to start putting back into the community until his company was a huge business. Over the years, two more Tim Hortons camps opened: one in Nova Scotia and another in the Canadian Rockies. (A fourth camp is scheduled to open July, 1994 in Quebec.) Ron's company flies in kids from all over the country so young Canadians in one part of Canada can learn what life is like in a very different part of that big country. They spend $700,000 per year just on airfare for the kids.

The reason Ron Joyce led the charge to build these camps is that he cares about the needs and futures of kids growing up poor. And don't you think that sponsoring these camps might make the donut customers just a little bit more loyal? Doing good usually finds its way back to the doer, even when it's not expected.

Well done, Ron Joyce!

Many people think that you should hold off on giving back to the community until you've made it big. A medium- or small-sized business can actually make a name for itself as a business by helping out the community first.

In fact, how many times in life do we pass up a chance to give first, before we are asked?

- To volunteer to head up the church picnic committee . . .

- To be the first to donate money when a child in the community needs a kidney transplant . . .

- To offer to watch a new neighbor's kids while they handle all those errands that go with moving in.

It's funny, but today that golf course is mostly important to me because of the charity tournament we play there. The course is a fine little business, but its biggest payback to me was that it helped me build a relationship with Governor Campbell, who has become a real ally on the adoption cause. And if that old yacht got traded and started a chain reaction so that just one more child has a home, this seagoing general in his dress whites thinks he cut a pretty good deal.

PAYING PETER TO PAY PAUL

Author Robert Fulghum tells a super story about V. P. Menon, a famous politician in India's history. One day Menon was in a strange city and thieves stole everything he had. A perfect stranger gave him some money and saved the day for the grateful traveler. There was a hitch: Menon had to pay back this money, not to the stranger who had lent him the cash, but to some other stranger Menon might some day run into who would be in need.[1]

---

1. Robert Fulghum, *All I Really Need to Know I Learned in Kindergarten* (New York: Villard, 1986), p. 153.

You should always encourage others to pay back what they borrowed from you, but not always to you. I thought about the V. P. Menon story as I read an article about Dr. Timothy Jones—a family practicioner who practices in Whitney Point, New York. Dr. Jones treats patients who can't afford to pay their doctor bills, but they still have to pay back for the services rendered. Instead of paying Dr. Jones, they have to do "X" hours of volunteer work in the community—maybe at a soup kitchen or doing maintenance for the school system.[2] I guess Doc Jones figures he's getting his share out of life already. Aren't most of us?

Generosity doesn't have to be any big thing. In fact, it would do us all good to study some of the neat little things that happen in small towns across America every day.

Ask Mike Toukan. He is a Wendy's franchisee out in Nebraska and the Dakotas. (If you watch Wendy's ads, you'd know Mike because he got cast not long ago as a biker wearing shades and a pirate's scarf wrapped around his head for one of the commercials. In real life, Mike is about as nice and soft-spoken as a person can get; he's never even ridden a motorcycle. His cameo role resulted from his being a top bidder in a charitable auciton supporting Wendy's Three-Tour Challenge.)

What can a business like a restaurant do in a small town to show that it cares?

- Set up a program that invites a star student and his or her parents to have dinner on the house.

- Donate some chili to the local halfway house.

- Put up crayon drawings from the grade school and hold a contest to pick the best sketch.

Sure, all the big national programs are nice, but if we lose sight of this kind of local giving, America will be a worse place for it. And our land's tradition has always been that we have

---

2. "Heroes for Today," *Reader's Digest*, November, 1993, p. 20.

never expected any of this generosity to come back. It's just a duty we have.

We all have heard of "vicious circles," and most of us have been trapped in a good number of them in our lives. But what if we get the arrow pointed in the other direction and start putting some "virtuous circles" into motion? Let's prod people to think of others—not just those to whom they may already feel indebted. You know, "I'll scratch your back. Now you go scratch somebody else's." Never let them repay you, but ask that they anonymously repay their debt to you to someone else. As I see it, with just a little sensible planning, the whole thing could easily get totally out of control. We'd be swallowed up by a tidal wave of people doing good things for others.

Wouldn't that be great?

A Final Word

THE ROAR OF THE CROWD

Dexter Yager, a major distributor with Amway—the famous marketing organization—asked me to give a talk to his people. Dexter was once a used-car salesman. He's still a salesman, a master salesman with hundreds of thousands of distributors within his organization. Maybe I should call him a marketer. A typical salesman comes and goes; the typical salesman does not think like Dexter. Dexter has staying power and knows people. But even Dex can make mistakes: Like what can I, Dave Thomas, teach Amway about succeeding that Amway doesn't already know?

The Yager celebration happened in Charlotte, North Carolina. Dexter and his wife Birdie took me out for a nice dinner. I wasn't supposed to talk until 9:30 that night. I knew that Dexter was having his main meeting over at the Charlotte Coliseum, where the Hornets basketball team plays. That place is *big*, and they were expecting a full house. The audience was distributors throughout the east coast and Canada. They didn't know who was speaking, it was supposed to be a surprise.

I was scared. Dexter was paying me $10,000 (which I would give to children's charities) to make this talk. After dinner, I went back to the hotel, paced the carpet until it started to pill, and asked myself, *How many amplifiers do you need for one human voice to drown out the drone of 23,000 people snoring? Do we still have time to rent the amps?*

I got so scared, in fact, I almost called up Dex right before nine, ready to tell him, "Dex, I will give you $15,000 if I *don't* have to speak tonight. Net profit: $5,000. Take the dough."

To tell the truth, I was too chicken *not* to show up. As I walked down the Coliseum ramp I felt like Sugar Ray Leonard heading into the ring, except I was sure I was going to be going down for the count. Actually, I felt more like the ancient Christians going up against the gladiators—except I didn't have near the confidence that those saints did.

Okay, so I do national T.V. Television is duck soup compared to 23,000 people live. You talk to a little red light when you tape a T.V. commercial. If you make a mistake, somebody says "Let's take it again." And they have people on the set in charge of sweat and everything else. Not so when you're the big act in some gigantic stadium.

When I got to the end of the ramp, something I didn't expect started up. The guy at the podium introducing me had hardly spoken my name when they just started screaming. For five minutes they just hollered and stomped. I couldn't even talk to the people. No snores. Just screams. They made me feel like the pope: I would just wave my hand and pat it down, and people would think they got blessed.

Finally they quieted down enough so that I could say, "You were cheering so much, I just want you to know that I haven't said anything. You may not want to cheer after you hear what I have to say." They roared again. It was almost like making an acceptance speech at a national political convention. I trusted my gut instincts and tore up my notes.

"Don't you want to make more money?"

Roar.

"Don't you believe in the free-enterprise system?"

Roar.

"Don't you think that people should do the right thing and be nice to each other?"

Roar.

It went on like that for a half an hour.

Taught me a lesson. For an ordinary person, the biggest key to being successful at making a speech is not having a great speech written up ahead of time. It's having a great audience. An everyday guy like me needs every break he can get.

A Great Goodbye

Among the people I've had the honor of knowing, the two greatest public speakers were surely Danny Thomas and Dr.

Norman Vincent Peale. They were also the two biggest personal success stories. I've told you about Danny. Let me tell you about Dr. Peale.

Norman Vincent Peale truly gave every nook and cranny of his soul and self for the sake of others. When he gave me the Horatio Alger Award in 1978, I know that he handed me the greatest single moment of my life. It was the one pat on the back that made whatever work I had done in my life all worth it.

For months my heart was set on closing this book with a conversation with Dr. Peale. God had other plans. Norman Vincent Peale passed away on Christmas Eve, 1993. He was ninety-five.

Dr. Peale had a great partner. He still does. Talk to his partner, and you'd sense in a shake that the spirit of what Dr. Peale was and is all about is just as alive as ever. Dr. Peale's partner in his dreams and his work is his bride, Mrs. Ruth Stafford Peale—and she has as much energy and grace as you could ever imagine in an eighty-seven-year-young woman. Talking with Mrs. Ruth is liking hearing Dr. Norman's voice. It's true now more than ever in all the years I have known the Peales.

During their life together, Team Peale paired two different strengths. Dr. Norman was the creative person, so Mrs. Ruth says, and she was the organizer. Mrs. Ruth knew one special secret about her husband. He could be as creative as anyone in the world, provided that *he dealt with just one thing at a time.* "If you put five things on his desk that needed to be done," Mrs. Ruth says, "a newspaper column, a bunch of letters, telephone calls, what-have-you, he'd often say, 'I'm not going to do any of this.' But if you gave him one thing at a time and would tell him that this column is due today, or encourage him to finish some other item, then he'd get it done very fast."

I can remember attending a board meeting for *Guideposts Magazine.* The meeting was being chaired by Mrs. Ruth, and Dr. Norman arrived late. As he came in the door, she said to him, "Norman, I know you'll want to pray now, and that's fine;

but why don't we think of it as kind of a brunch prayer—one prayer good for breakfast and one for lunch, too, since we're running so far behind on our agenda." Mrs. Ruth steered Dr. Norman's strengths to make them shine as bright as they could, and she spent her whole life doing it. My creativity can't hold a candle compared to Dr. Norman's, but I count myself lucky that my wife Lorraine has helped me so often by organizing so much in my life and putting everything in our family and home in ship-shape order.

Dr. Norman loved to give talks. It seemed that no audience ever gave Norman Vincent Peale the jitters. He thrived on being able to lift big crowds up, to give them the right attitude. While most of us—almost *all* of us—need a friendly, warmed-up audience to give a good talk, Dr. Norman had the gift of taking any audience and making it *his* audience.

When he was ninety-four, he made his last big speech at the yearly commencement of Ohio Wesleyan University. He talked for twenty-five minutes without a single note in front of two thousand people. It was a red-letter day for Dr. Norman—seventy-two years almost to the hour after receiving his own diploma from the same college.

Mrs. Ruth said he grew weaker after that big event. Over the days and months that followed, he stayed at home mostly and the strength kind of went out of him day by day—the strength, but not the spirit. Not the fun either. One morning their daughter Margaret was helping to feed Dr. Norman. His eyes lit up—as only Dr. Norman's could—and he said in a clear voice, *"No more oatmeal!!!"*

At his farm in Pawling, New York, at four o'clock in the afternoon on Christmas Eve, the family gathered in his room. He was very, very weak. The children and the grandchildren were there. This time Dr. Norman was the audience. His family gave *him* a speech from their hearts. Mrs. Ruth says that the family stood around his bed, and they told him how much they loved him and how much *he* had inspired them. Then she said, "Finally, quietly, and just slowly, his breathing became a little bit less, and he just gave his last breath. There was no pain. There was no struggle. It was the most natural experience that you could possibly describe."

When I heard that story, all I could say was, "What a wonderful end to such a perfect life." There were no tears in Mrs. Ruth's voice. All she did was nod and say, "Isn't that *great?*" Then she added that she was sure Dr. Peale organized a talk for the angels in heaven that Christmas Eve. I bet he did, and I bet he brought the house down, too.

"Well done, thou good and faithful servant!"

Well done, Dr. Norman Vincent Peale, and every person like him—ordinary and extraordinary—who has decided that doing the right thing is what this life is all about.

INDEX